Wok &
Stir-Fry

Wok & Stir-Fry

David Lee

St Michael
FROM
MARKS & SPENCER

This edition first published in the U.K. in 1997
by Kitchen Library an imprint of Hamlyn
for Marks and Spencer p.l.c.
Baker Street, London
England

Copyright © 1997 Reed International Books Limited

Printed in China

NOTES

Both metric and imperial measurements have been given in all recipes. Use one set of measurements only and not a mixture of both.

Standard level spoon measurements are used in all recipes.
1 tablespoon = one 15 ml spoon
1 teaspoon = one 5 ml spoon

Eggs should be size 3 unless otherwise stated.
The Department of Health advises that eggs should not be consumed raw. This book contains dishes made with raw or lightly cooked eggs. It is prudent for more vulnerable people such as pregnant and nursing mothers, invalids, the elderly, babies and young children to avoid uncooked or lightly cooked dishes made with eggs. Once prepared, these dishes should be kept refrigerated and used promptly.

Meat and poultry should be cooked thoroughly. To test if poultry is cooked, pierce the flesh through the thickest part with a skewer or fork – the juices should run clear, never pink or red. Do not re-freeze poultry that has been frozen previously and thawed.
Do not re-freeze a cooked dish that has been frozen previously.

Milk should be full fat unless otherwise stated.

Nut and Nut derivatives.
This book includes dishes made with nuts and nut derivatives. It is advisable for customers with known allergic reactions to nuts and nut derivatives and those who may be potentially vulnerable to these allergies, such as pregnant and nursing mothers, invalids, the elderly, babies and young children to avoid dishes made with nuts and nut oils. It is also prudent to check the labels of pre-prepared ingredients for the possible inclusion of nut derivatives.

Pepper should be freshly ground black pepper unless otherwise stated.

Fresh herbs should be used, unless otherwise stated. If unavailable, use dried herbs as an alternative but halve the quantities stated.

Measurements for canned food have been given as a standard metric equivalent.

Contents

Introduction

Stir-frying is a cooking technique which has long been used throughout South-east Asia and is now very popular in Western cooking, too. This is partly because it is a quick and simple way to cook foods, ideally suited to people with busy lifestyles, but also because it is a very healthy form of cooking, during which meats, fish, rice and vegetables lose very few important minerals and vitamins.

Stir-frying involves cooking food very quickly in oil heated to a high temperature, with seasonings and optional sauces, stocks and wine. Since the amount of oil used in most stir-frying recipes is minimal, it is a technique which could more properly be described as 'cooking with oil', rather than 'cooking in oil'.

You will find in this book a wide and deliciously varied selection of wok and stir-fry recipes, many of them based on the different cooking styles of South-east Asia, from China to Malaysia, and with others showing a distinctive Western influence on the choice of ingredients.

There are chapters on cooking with chicken and duck, with meat, pork and lamb, with fish and shellfish, with vegetables and with noodles and rice.

Vegetarians will find plenty to interest them in the last two chapters.

USING A WOK

While stir-frying can be done successfully in a heavy-based frying pan, the ideal utensil is still the widely-used Asian cooking pan, the wok, which can also be used for steaming, braising and deep-frying. The wok's rounded bottom and curved sides allows foods to be pushed up the sides and out of the oil, which drains off the food and back down to the base of the wok, while the food still cooks in the heat of the pan.

In the Western kitchen the wok is most easily used on gas cookers, because the heat can be adjusted much more quickly than on electric ones. You can buy special rings to keep the wok steady on gas rings.

If you think you will be doing a lot of wok cookery, it is a good idea to have two woks, a big, two-handled one with a lid for deep-frying and steaming, and a smaller, one-handled one for stir-frying. A wok rack, which sits over one half of the wok, is useful because you can drain cooked foods on it while continuing to cook other food in the wok. You will be using both hands when stir-frying, one to hold the wok's handle, and the other to stir the food constantly with a spatula or chopsticks as it cooks.

WOK COOKERY UTENSILS

Besides the wok itself, other utensils it is useful to have when cooking with a wok, include a *wok rack*, which fits on to the wok rim to hold pieces of food during cooking and to drain food once it has been cooked; a *slotted spoon* or *skimmer* for lifting cooked foods out of the wok; and several *wooden spatulas* (or chopsticks) for stirring the food in the wok. Thai cooks also have a large mesh *frying basket*, for lowering foods into hot oil for deep-frying.

For preparing food for wok cookery,

you should have one or two solid wooden *chopping boards*; several *good sharp knives,* including a thin bladed knife for shredding, slicing and dicing, a heavy knife for cutting meat very finely and a knife for cutting through the bones and joints of poultry; and a *pestle and mortar* so that you can have a supply of freshly ground spices at all times. A pestle and mortar is also ideal for making things like garlic mixture (see right).

PREPARING A NEW WOK

While non-stick and stainless steel woks are available, the traditional Chinese wok, made of iron, is still the most popular among dedicated stir-fry cooks. A new iron wok is always sold coated with oil or a wax film to stop it rusting. To prepare it for use, you must remove this film:

• Heat the wok over a high heat until it is very hot indeed, then scrub it in warm, soapy water with a stiff brush and rinse it thoroughly. Dry the wok by putting it over a moderate heat.

• Now you must season the wok, to prevent it rusting and to stop food sticking to it during cooking. To do this, simply wipe over the entire inside surface of the dry wok with a pad of kitchen paper soaked in cooking oil.

• To preserve the seasoning, do not wash the wok in detergent after use. Use just hot water, plus a stiff brush or non-abrasive scourer to scrape off any food stuck to the base. Repeat the seasoning process after washing the wok, so that it develops a smooth, shiny surface.

SUCCESSFUL STIR-FRYING

• Foods must be properly prepared in advance, trimmed and cut into similarly sized and shaped pieces so that they cook evenly.

• The wok should be preheated before the oil, which should be a good quality light oil, is added. Heat the oil until it is smoking, allow it to cool slightly (until it is sizzling), then add the food.

• Keep the heat high during cooking, so that the overall cooking time is a short one.

• Ingredients which need longer cooking should be put into the wok first: for this reason, you should carefully follow the order of cooking set out in the recipe methods in this book.

• The food should be stirred and moved vigorously in the wok all the time it is cooking, using chopsticks or a spatula.

• Never over-cook stir-fried food: it should be tender but still with a crisp texture, and a fresh colour. Serve it as soon as it is ready.

SOME BASIC RECIPES

These recipes are for basic stocks and mixtures, used in wide variety of oriental dishes, which you will find in many of the recipes in this book.

COCONUT MILK AND CREAM

Mix 400 g/14 oz grated or desiccated coconut with 900 ml/1½ pints milk in a saucepan, bring to the boil, then lower the heat and simmer, stirring occasionally, until the mixture is reduced by one third. Strain, extracting as much liquid as possible. Pour the strained milk into a bowl and chill in the refrigerator. When it is cold, skim off the thicker 'cream' that rises to the surface. The remaining liquid is the coconut milk.

Coconut Milk goes well with shellfish; in this book it is used in Prawn Curry (see page 50) and Prawns in Coconut Sauce (see page 51)

GARLIC MIXTURE

Put 2 tablespoons of crushed garlic, 2 tablespoons chopped coriander stem and ½ teaspoon pepper into a mortar and pound to a paste.

This pungent mixture gives an extra tang to fish dishes, such as Seafood in Batter (see page 59).

GREEN CURRY PASTE

Remove the stems and seeds from 6 dried green chillies. Place in a food processor and work to a smooth paste with 3 tablespoons chopped spring onions, 1 tablespoon chopped garlic, 1 tablespoon chopped lemon grass, 1 tablespoon shrimp paste, 1 teaspoon ground laos, 1 teaspoon caraway seeds, 2 teaspoons coriander seeds, 1 teaspoon finely grated lemon rind and 1 teaspoon salt. Store in a screw-top jar in the refrigerator for up to 3 weeks.

Green Curry Paste is an excellent base for fish dishes and in this book is used in, for example, Prawn Curry (see page 50).

RED CURRY PASTE

Deseed 6 dried red chillies and soak them in water for 10 minutes. Drain

USING WONTON WRAPPERS

1 The wrappers, spread on a lightly floured surface and with a good spoonful of filling in the middle, are made into little 'bags' by lifting up the four corners and drawing them into the middle, over the filling.

2 The corners of the little bags are held together with chive ties: choose fairly thick chives, about 10 cm/4 inches long, which will not break easily.

3 The little bags are deep-fried, a few at a time, in hot oil, until they are crisp and golden brown. (Too many fried together would reduce the heat of the oil and make the bags soggy.) A slotted spoon or skimmer is used to lift the bags out of the hot fat.

well and chop roughly. Place in a food processor and work to a smooth paste with 2 tablespoons chopped lemon grass, 1 tablespoon chopped shallot, 1 tablespoon chopped garlic, 1 tablespoon chopped coriander stem, 1 teaspoon chopped galangal, 2 teaspoons coriander seeds, 1 teaspoon cumin seeds, 6 white peppercorns, 1 teaspoon salt and 1 teaspoon shrimp paste. Store in a screwtop jar in the refrigerator for up to 3 weeks.

Spicy Fishcakes (see page 61) are made specially delicious by the addition of Red Curry Paste.

FRIED ONION RINGS

Heat about 300 ml/½ pint vegetable oil in a wok or deep-fat fryer until hot but not smoking, add 1 large thinly sliced onion and deep-fry for 3–4 minutes, until golden brown. Remove from the

pan with a slotted spoon and drain on kitchen paper. Serve hot or at room temperature.

These Fried Onion Rings make a good garnish. You'll find them used in Nasi Goreng (see page 94), for instance.

WONTON WRAPPERS

Wafer-thin wonton wrappers, or skins, are made from wheat flour, egg and water and are sold in 8 cm/3 inch squares. In Chinese cooking they can be deep-fried on their own and served with a piquant dip, but they are more often filled with a savoury mixture and steamed, boiled or deep-fried. The step-by-step sequence above shows how easily they can be used to make such delicious starters as the Fried Golden Bags on page 41. Other fillings which could be used with wonton

wrappers are those given in the recipes for Deep-fried Wontons (see page 37) and Crab Rolls (see page 57).

SPRING ROLLS

Spring Rolls have long been a popular starter in Chinese restaurants. Basically, they are pancakes, wrapped round a tasty filling, in which bean sprouts are often included, as in the recipe on page 40.

The step-by-step sequence above takes you through the steps of filling, folding and frying the rolls:

GARNISHING WOK AND STIR-FRY DISHES

Many different garnishes, including fresh herbs, nuts, seeds and vegetable pieces have been used to put simple yet effective finishing touches to recipes in this book. To extend the Far

MAKING SPRING ROLLS

1 A freshly-made pancake is laid on a working surface and 2–3 tablespoonfuls of the filling are placed in the centre.

2 The sides of the pancake are folded in over the filling and the pancake is rolled up from the top. The edges, especially the long edge at the end of the roll-up, are sealed with a flour and water paste (1 tablespoon of plain flour mixed to a paste with 1 tablespoon of water). This prevents the filling seeping out during cooking.

3 Sufficient oil to deep-fry the Spring Rolls is heated in a wok to 180°–190°C/350°–375°F. The Spring Rolls are fried until a light golden colour then removed from the oil and drained on kitchen paper.

Eastern style of your cooking, try using these typical oriental garnishes.

RED CHILLI FLOWERS

Using a sharp, pointed knife, cut the chilli lengthways into 4 sections, slicing from the base to the tip, being careful not to cut right through the base. With the point of the knife, scrape out the chilli seeds, then drop the chillies into a bowl of iced water and place in the refrigerator for at least 30 minutes, until the sections of the chilli open out like a flower. Drain well before use.

CUCUMBER OR LEMON SLICES

Finely cut cucumber and lemon slices, used either flat or as curls, make an attractive garnish. Use the notch on a canelle knife to remove strips of skin at regular intervals down a cucumber or lemon before cutting them into even, thin slices. (Remove any pips from lemon slices). For curls, make a cut from the edge of the slice to the centre, then twist the two cut edges away from each other.

RADISH ROSES

Remove the stalk from the radish and, using the point of a small sharp knife, cut a row of petal shapes round the radish, keeping them joined at the base. Cut a second row of petal shapes in between and above the first row. Continue cutting rows of petal shapes until the top of the radish is reached. Place the radish rose in iced water for several hours to open out.

SPRING ONION TASSELS

Using a small sharp knife, remove and discard the root from the spring onion and and trim the stem to about 7.5 cm (3 inches) long. Cut lengthways through the green stalk several times to within 4 cm (1½ inches) of the end. Place in iced water for about 1 hour to open out.

TOMATO ROSE

Use a firm tomato to make this garnish. With a sharp knife, remove the skin in one continuous strip about 1 cm (½ inch) wide, starting at the smooth end. With the flesh side inside, start to curl the strip of tomato skin from the base end, forming a bud shape. Continue winding the strip of skin into a rose.

Chicken and Duck

Oriental Chicken with Turmeric

100 g/3 ½ oz creamed coconut, roughly chopped	8 chicken thighs, boned, skinned and cut into large chunks
50 g/2 oz macadamia nuts, roughly chopped	1 tablespoon turmeric
1 garlic clove, roughly chopped	1 teaspoon serai powder
3 tablespoons vegetable oil	thinly pared rind and juice of 1 lemon
1 onion, finely chopped	salt and pepper
	sprigs of flat leaf parsley, to garnish

1 Put the chopped coconut into a measuring jug, pour in boiling water up to the 300 ml/ ½ pint mark and stir until the coconut is dissolved. Set aside.

2 Pound half of the macadamia nuts to a paste with the garlic using a mortar and pestle, or work in a food processor. Heat the oil in the wok over moderate heat. Add the onion together with the nut and garlic paste and stir-fry for 2–3 minutes or until the onion is softened, taking care not to let it brown.

3 Add the chicken pieces, increase the heat to high and stir-fry for 1–2 minutes or until the chicken is lightly coloured on all sides. Stir in the turmeric and serai powder and salt and pepper to taste. Add the coconut milk and bring to the boil, stirring constantly.

4 Lower the heat, add the lemon rind and juice and simmer for about 10 minutes or until the chicken is tender and the sauce thickened, stirring frequently to prevent sticking. Remove and discard the lemon rind. Taste for seasoning and serve hot, sprinkled with the remaining chopped macadamia nuts and flat leaf parsley sprigs.

Serves 3–4

Preparation time: 20 minutes
Cooking time: about 30 minutes

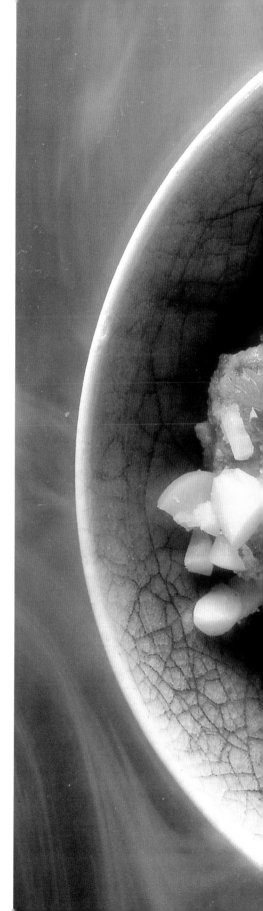

Chicken with Walnuts

- 300 g–375 g/10–12 oz boneless, skinless chicken breasts, cut into small cubes
- ½ teaspoon salt
- 1 egg white
- 1 tablespoon cornflour plus 1 teaspoon
- 4 tablespoons vegetable oil
- 2 spring onions, cut into 1 cm/½ inch lengths
- 2 slices fresh root ginger, peeled and cut into strips
- 3–4 dried red chillies, deseeded and thinly sliced
- 50 g/2 oz shelled walnuts, rough chopped
- 1 tablespoon yellow or black bean sauce
- 1 green pepper, cored, deseeded and cut into chunks
- 1 teaspoon sugar
- 2 tablespoons dry sherry
- 1 tablespoon cold water

1 Place the chicken in a bowl with the salt, and mix in the egg white and 1 tablespoon of the cornflour.
2 Heat the oil in the wok and add the chicken cubes. Stir-fry briskly for a few minutes until the colour changes from pink to white. Remove from the wok with a slotted spoon and set aside.
3 Add the spring onions, ginger, chillies and walnuts to the hot oil in the wok, and then stir in the yellow or black bean sauce. Stir a few times and then add the green pepper. Return the chicken to the wok and stir well. Add the sugar and sherry, and stir-fry for about 1 minute.
4 Mix the remaining teaspoon of corn-flour to a smooth paste with the water. Add this mixture to the wok and blend well until thickened. Transfer to a warm serving dish and serve at once.

Serves 3–4
Preparation time: 15 minutes
Cooking time: 5 minutes

Shredded Chicken and Celery

- 250 g/8 oz boneless, skinless chicken breasts, cut into shreds
- ½ teaspoon salt
- 1 egg white
- 1 tablespoon cornflour
- 4 tablespoons vegetable oil
- 4 slices fresh root ginger, peeled and cut into thin strips
- 2 spring onions, cut into thin strips
- 1 small celery stick, cut into strips
- 1 green pepper, cored, deseeded and cut into thin strips
- 2 tablespoons soy sauce
- 1 tablespoon dry sherry

1 Place the chicken in a bowl. Add the salt, egg white and cornflour and mix thoroughly.

2 Heat the oil in the wok and add the chicken shreds. Stir-fry over moderate heat until the chicken is lightly and evenly coloured. Remove the chicken with a slotted spoon and set aside.

3 Increase the heat and, when the oil is very hot, add the ginger and spring onions followed by the celery and green pepper. Stir-fry for about 30 seconds over high heat.

4 Return the chicken shreds to the wok with the soy sauce and sherry. Mix well and cook for a further 1–1½ minutes, stirring all the time. Transfer to a serving dish and serve immediately.

Serves 3–4

Preparation time: 15 minutes
Cooking time: 7–8 minutes

Chicken Curry

- 150 g/5 oz creamed coconut, roughly chopped
- 150 ml/¼ pint water
- 4 large boneless, skinless chicken breasts, sliced
- 1 aubergine, peeled, cubed and blanched
- 2.5 cm/1 inch piece fresh root ginger, peeled and chopped
- 2–3 kaffir lime leaves, torn

CURRY PASTE:
- ½ teaspoon roasted coriander seeds
- 1 stalk lemon grass, finely chopped
- grated rind of 1 lime
- 2 fresh green chillies, deseeded and chopped
- 1 teaspoon cumin seeds
- 1 teaspoon shrimp paste
- 3 garlic cloves, crushed
- 1 small onion, finely chopped

TO SERVE:
- fresh basil leaves
- 1 green chilli, deseeded and cut into strips

1 Put the creamed coconut and water into the wok and heat gently, stirring all the time, until the coconut melts. Add the chicken and simmer for 10 minutes. Remove the chicken with a slotted spoon and keep warm. Reserve the coconut liquid.

2 To make the curry paste, grind all the ingredients to a smooth paste using a pestle and mortar. Alternatively, blend them in a food processor or blender at high speed until smooth.

3 Add the curry paste to the reserved coconut liquid and heat gently, stirring constantly. Continue stirring over low heat until the liquid starts to evaporate and thicken.

4 Add the reserved chicken, cubed aubergine, ginger and kaffir lime leaves and cook gently for a few minutes. Serve the curry sprinkled with basil leaves and green chilli strips, with noodles or boiled rice.

Serves 4
Preparation time: 10 minutes
Cooking time: 30 minutes

Ginger Chicken with Honey

- 5 spring onions, sliced into 1 cm/½ inch pieces
- 50 g/2 oz fresh root ginger, peeled and finely chopped
- 2 tablespoons vegetable oil
- 3 boneless, skinless chicken breasts, sliced thinly
- 3 chicken livers, chopped
- 2 tablespoons dried Chinese black mushrooms, soaked in warm water for 20 minutes
- 1 onion, sliced
- 3 garlic cloves, crushed
- 2 tablespoons soy sauce
- 1 tablespoon honey

1 Put the spring onions into a bowl, cover with cold water and leave to soak until required. Mix the chopped ginger with a little cold water, then drain and squeeze to remove its hotness. Rinse under cold running water and drain well.

2 Heat the oil in the wok over moderate heat. Add the chicken with the chicken livers. Stir-fry for 5 minutes, then remove with a slotted spoon and set aside.

3 Drain the mushrooms and squeeze them dry. Discard the stalks. Add the onion to the wok and fry gently until soft. Add the garlic and mushrooms and stir-fry for 1 minute. Return the cooked chicken pieces and chicken livers to the wok.

4 Mix the soy sauce and honey, stirring until blended. Pour over the chicken

and stir well. Add the drained ginger and stir-fry for 2–3 minutes. Add the drained spring onions, and transfer to a serving dish. This dish tastes even better if it is cooked the day before and then reheated.

Serves 4
Preparation time: 15 minutes
Cooking time: 15 minutes

Lemon Chicken

This classic dish, which originated in Hong Kong, is simplicity itself to make. Spring onions are included to add crunch to the dish, but they are not essential. If you prefer, you can use green pepper instead, or leave out the vegetables altogether.

- 1 egg white
- 2 teaspoons cornflour
- pinch of salt
- 2 boneless, skinless chicken breasts, cut into thin strips across the grain
- 300 ml/½ pint vegetable oil
- ½ bunch of spring onions, shredded
- 1 garlic clove, crushed
- lemon slices, to garnish

SAUCE:

- 2 teaspoons cornflour
- cold chicken stock or water
- finely grated rind of ½ lemon
- 2 tablespoons lemon juice
- 1 tablespoon soy sauce
- 2 teaspoons rice wine or dry sherry
- 2 teaspoons caster sugar

1 First prepare the sauce. Mix the cornflour to a thin paste with the stock or water, then stir in the remaining sauce ingredients. Set aside.

2 Lightly beat the egg white in a shallow dish with the cornflour and salt. Add the strips of chicken and turn to coat. Set aside.

3 Heat the oil in the wok until hot but not smoking. Lift the strips of chicken one at a time out of the egg white mixture with a fork and drop into the hot oil. Shallow-fry in batches for about 3–4 minutes, or until golden. Remove with a slotted spoon and drain on kitchen paper. Keep hot.

4 Pour off all but 1 tablespoon of the oil from the wok. Add the spring onions and garlic and stir-fry over a moderate heat for 30 seconds. Stir the sauce, pour into the wok and stir to mix. Increase the heat to high and bring to the boil, stirring constantly.

5 Return the chicken to the wok and stir-fry for 1–2 minutes or until evenly coated in the sauce. Serve at once, garnished with lemon slices.

Serves 2

Preparation time: 20 minutes
Cooking time: about 25 minutes

Szechuan Pepper Chicken

Szechuan dishes are often hot and spicy. This recipe uses bottled chilli sauce to create instant heat. You can add more to taste, if you like, taking into account the 'hotness' of the brand you are using.

- 4 tablespoons water
- 2 tablespoons hot chilli sauce, or to taste
- 1 tablespoon soy sauce
- 2 tablespoons vegetable oil
- 2–4 spring onions, thinly sliced on the diagonal
- 5 cm/2 inch piece fresh root ginger, peeled and finely chopped
- 1 garlic clove, crushed
- 4 boneless, skinless chicken breasts, cut into thin strips across the grain
- spring onions, to garnish (optional)

1 Mix the water with the hot chilli sauce and soy sauce in a jug or bowl. Set aside.

2 Heat the oil in the wok over moderate heat. Add the spring onions, ginger and garlic and stir-fry for 30 seconds. Add the chicken strips, increase the heat to high and stir-fry for 3–4 minutes or until lightly coloured on all sides.

3 Add the chilli sauce mixture and toss until all the ingredients are well combined and piping hot. Serve at once, garnished with spring onions, if liked.

Serves 3–4
Preparation time: 20 minutes
Cooking time: 10 minutes

Five-Spice Chicken

Five-spice powder is available from the spice racks of supermarkets and in oriental stores. A combination of five ground spices – star anise, cinnamon, cloves, fennel seed and Szechuan peppercorns – it is used extensively in both Chinese and Malaysian cooking. Aromatic rather than hot and spicy, it goes well with the delicate flavour of chicken.

- 3 tablespoons vegetable oil
- 4 boneless, skinless, chicken breasts, cut into thin strips across the grain
- 1 onion, thinly sliced
- 3 carrots, cut into julienne strips
- 125 g/4 oz cauliflower florets, divided into tiny sprigs
- 1½ teaspoons five-spice powder
- 75 ml/3 fl oz chicken stock or water
- 2 tablespoons soy sauce
- 1 x 225 g/7½ oz can water chestnuts, drained and sliced
- pepper

1 Heat the oil in the wok over a moderate heat. Add the chicken strips, increase the heat to high and stir-fry for 3–4 minutes or until lightly coloured on all sides. Remove the wok from the heat and transfer the chicken strips to a plate with a slotted spoon. Set aside.

2 Add the onion, carrots and cauliflower to the wok and sprinkle over the five-spice powder. Stir-fry for 3–4 minutes or until softened, taking care not to let the vegetables brown. Add the stock or water and soy sauce and stir until bubbling.

3 Return the chicken and its juices to the wok and add the water chestnuts. Toss for 1–2 minutes or until all the ingredients are well combined and piping hot. Add pepper to taste and serve immediately.

Serves 3–4

Preparation time: 15 minutes
Cooking time: about 15 minutes

Stir-fried Sesame Chicken

- 500 g/1 lb boneless, skinless chicken breasts, cut into 2.5 cm/1 inch cubes
- 1½ teaspoons cornflour
- 4 tablespoons vegetable oil
- 1 green pepper, cored, deseeded and cut into 2.5 cm/1 inch pieces
- 2½ tablespoons soy sauce
- 2½ tablespoons sesame seed paste
- 1 tablespoon sesame oil
- 1 tablespoon stock or water
- 1 teaspoon chilli sauce
- 1 tablespoon dry sherry
- sesame seeds, to garnish

1 Put the chicken cubes into a bowl, sprinkle with the cornflour and toss until they are evenly coated. Heat the oil in the wok and add the chicken. Stir-fry over high heat for 45 seconds, then remove from the wok with a slotted spoon and set aside.

2 Add the green pepper to the hot oil in the wok and stir-fry briskly over moderate heat for 1 minute. Stir in 1 tablespoon of the soy sauce, then remove the green pepper with a slotted spoon and set aside.

3 Add the remaining soy sauce, the sesame seed paste, sesame oil, stock or water, chilli sauce and sherry. Mix together well and cook for 1 minute.

4 Return the chicken cubes to the sauce mixture in the wok and stir over high heat for about 45 seconds. Stir in the reserved green pepper. Cook for a further 30 seconds until the pepper is just tender. Transfer to a serving dish and serve immediately, garnished with the sesame seeds.

Serves 3–4

Preparation time: 10 minutes
Cooking time: 7–8 minutes

Fried Eight-piece Chicken

- 2–3 spring onions, finely chopped
- 2–3 slices fresh root ginger, peeled and finely chopped
- 2 tablespoons dry sherry
- 1 tablespoon sugar
- 3 tablespoons soy sauce
- 1 x 1.25 kg/2½ lb spring chicken, jointed and breasts cut in half
- 3 tablespoons cornflour
- 4 tablespoons vegetable oil
- 1 teaspoon sesame oil
- chopped chives, to garnish

1 In a large bowl, mix together the spring onions and ginger with 1 tablespoon of the sherry, 1 teaspoon of the sugar and 1 tablespoon of the soy sauce. Add the chicken pieces and turn in the marinade until well coated. Leave to marinate for about 5 minutes.
2 Remove the chicken from the marinade and coat each piece with cornflour, reserving any leftover marinade. Meanwhile, heat the oil in the wok.
3 Add the chicken to the wok and fry over moderate heat until golden brown all over and cooked through. Pour off the excess oil from the wok and add the remaining sherry, sugar, soy sauce and leftover marinade. Bring to the boil, stirring. Stir in the sesame oil, then serve the chicken pieces immediately, garnished with chives.

Serves 4
Preparation time: 20 minutes
Cooking time: 15 minutes

Bang Bang Chicken

- 4 chicken breasts, boned and skinned
- 6 tablespoons soy sauce
- 2 tablespoons sesame oil
- 2.5 cm/1 inch piece fresh root ginger, peeled and finely chopped
- 2 tablespoons sesame seeds
- 4 tablespoons vegetable oil
- 4 carrots, cut into julienne strips
- 1 fresh green or red chilli, deseeded and chopped
- 125 g/4 oz bean sprouts
- ½ cucumber, cut into julienne strips
- 3 tablespoons rice wine or dry sherry
- 2 tablespoons clear honey
- 150 ml/¼ pint chicken stock
- flat leaf parsley, to garnish

1 Place the chicken between 2 sheets of greaseproof paper and bang hard with a rolling pin to flatten and tenderize them. Cut the chicken into thin strips across the grain, then place in a shallow dish. Mix 2 tablespoons of the soy sauce with the sesame oil and ginger. Pour over the chicken and turn to coat. Cover and leave to marinate for 20 minutes, turning occasionally.

2 Meanwhile, heat the wok until hot. Add the sesame seeds and dry-fry over a gentle heat for 1–2 minutes or until toasted, tossing so they do not burn. Remove the wok from the heat and tip the seeds on to a plate. Set aside.

3 Return the wok to a moderate heat with 2 tablespoons of the vegetable oil. Add the carrots and chilli and stir-fry for 2–3 minutes. Remove with a slot-ted spoon and place in a bowl. Add the bean sprouts to the wok and stir-fry for 1 minute, then tip the bean sprouts into the bowl. Add the cucumber strips to the bowl and toss well.

4 Heat the remaining oil in the wok. Add the chicken, increase the heat and stir-fry for 4–5 minutes. Transfer the chicken to a separate bowl.

5 Add the remaining soy sauce, the rice wine or sherry, honey and stock to the wok. Bring to the boil, stirring, then simmer for a few minutes, stirring constantly, until reduced slightly. Pour half of the sauce mixture over the vegetables and half over the chicken. Stir to mix, then cover and leave to cool, stirring occasionally.

6 Arrange the chicken and vegetables on individual plates, drizzle over any sauce remaining in the bowls and sprinkle with the sesame seeds. Garnish with parsley and serve.

Serves 4

Preparation time: about 30 minutes, plus cooling

Cooking time: about 15 minutes

Plum Duck

- 2 tablespoons vegetable oil
- 4 duck breast fillets, about 175 g/6 oz each, skinned and cut into thin strips across the grain
- 250 g/8 oz red plums, stoned and thinly sliced
- finely grated rind and juice of 1 large orange
- 2 tablespoons port
- 2 tablespoons red wine vinegar
- 2 teaspoons soft brown sugar
- ¼ teaspoon ground cinnamon
- salt and pepper
- sprigs of thyme, to garnish

1 Heat the oil in the wok over moderate heat until hot. Add the duck strips, increase the heat to high and stir-fry for 3–4 minutes or until lightly coloured on all sides. Remove the wok from the heat and transfer the duck to a plate with a slotted spoon. Set aside.

2 Return the wok to a moderate heat. Add the plums, orange rind and juice, port, wine vinegar, sugar, cinnamon and salt and pepper to taste. Stir-fry for 5 minutes, then return the duck and its juices to the wok and increase the heat to high.

3 Toss for 1–2 minutes or until all the ingredients are combined and piping hot. Taste for seasoning and serve at once, garnished with sprigs of thyme.

Serves 3–4
Preparation time: 15 minutes
Cooking time: 15 minutes

VARIATION

Cherry Duck

Replace the plums, orange, port, vinegar, sugar and cinnamon with 1 x 500 g/ 1 lb can of pitted dark sweet cherries. Mix 1 tablespoon arrowroot with 4 tablespoons water. Cook the duck as for the main recipe. Fry 1 sliced onion with a 2.5 cm/1 inch piece of shredded ginger for 2–3 minutes until soft. Drain the cherries, reserving 4 tablespoons of the juice. Add the juice and the grated rind and juice of ½ lemon to the wok, season and bring to the boil. Stir in the arrowroot paste until thickened. Add the duck, its juices and the cherries and stir-fry for 1–2 minutes.

Duck with Spiced Orange Sauce

Boneless duck breasts and other duck portions are now readily available from large supermarkets.

- 2 tablespoons vegetable oil
- 4 duck breast fillets, about 175 g/6 oz each, skinned and cut into thin strips across the grain
- seeds of 6 cardamom pods, crushed
- pepper
- boiled or steamed rice, to serve
- orange segments, to garnish

SAUCE:
- 1 tablespoon cornflour
- 4 tablespoons water
- juice of 1 large orange
- 1 tablespoon rice wine or dry sherry
- 1 tablespoon soy sauce
- 1 teaspoon dark soft brown sugar
- 1 teaspoon five-spice powder

1 First prepare the sauce. Mix the cornflour to a thin paste with the water, then stir in the orange juice, rice wine or sherry, soy sauce, sugar and five-spice powder. Set aside.

2 Heat the oil in the wok over moderate heat until hot. Add the duck strips and crushed cardamom seeds, increase the heat to high and stir-fry for 3–4 minutes or until lightly coloured on all sides.

3 Stir the sauce to mix, then pour into the wok and bring to the boil, stirring constantly. Stir-fry for a further 1–2 minutes or until the duck is tender and coated in the sauce. Add

pepper to taste and serve at once with plain boiled or steamed rice, garnished with orange segments.

Serves 3–4
Preparation time: 10 minutes
Cooking time: 15 minutes

Beef, Pork and Lamb

Ginger Beef with Peppers

500 g/1 lb lean fillet steak, thinly sliced

2 teaspoons soy sauce

2 tablespoons sesame oil

2.5 cm/1 inch piece fresh root ginger, peeled and sliced

2 teaspoons vinegar

1 tablespoon water

1 teaspoon salt

1 teaspoon cornflour

1 garlic clove, crushed

pinch of five-spice powder

1 red pepper, cored, deseeded and cut into chunks

1 green pepper, cored, deseeded and cut into chunks

TO GARNISH:

slivers of fresh red chilli, deseeded

1 Put the slices of fillet steak into a bowl and add the soy sauce, 1 teaspoon of the sesame oil, the sliced ginger, vinegar, water, salt and cornflour. Stir well to mix, until the slices are coated thoroughly. Cover and leave to marinate in the refrigerator for at least 20 minutes.

2 Heat the remaining sesame oil in the wok and add the garlic and five-spice powder. Stir-fry for 30 seconds and then add the marinated steak slices. Stir-fry quickly until the meat is browned on the outside yet still pink and tender on the inside. Remove with a slotted spoon and set aside.

3 Add the red and green peppers to the wok and stir-fry briskly for 2–3 minutes, tossing them in the oil.

4 Add the steak and any remaining marinade. Stir-fry for 1 minute until the meat is heated through. Transfer to a serving dish and serve garnished with thin slivers of chilli.

Serves 3–4

Preparation time: 10 minutes

Cooking time: 5 minutes

Beef with Pineapple

- 500 g/1 lb rump or fillet steak, cut into thin strips
- 2 teaspoons cornflour
- 4 tablespoons cold beef stock or water
- 2 tablespoons rice wine or dry sherry
- 2 teaspoons dark soft brown sugar
- 3 tablespoons vegetable oil
- 3 celery sticks, thinly sliced on the diagonal
- 4 slices fresh pineapple, cubed
- salt and pepper

MARINADE:
- 2.5 cm/1 inch piece fresh root ginger, finely chopped
- 2 tablespoons vegetable oil
- 2 tablespoons soy sauce
- 1 tablespoon red wine vinegar
- ¼ teaspoon five-spice powder

1 To make the marinade, put all the ingredients into a dish, add the beef strips and turn to coat. Cover and marinate for 30 minutes, turning the beef occasionally.
2 Mix the cornflour to a thin paste with the stock or water, then stir in the rice wine or sherry and the sugar. Set aside.
3 Heat 2 tablespoons of the oil in the wok. Add the beef and marinade, increase the heat and stir-fry for 3–4 minutes. Tip the beef and its juices into a bowl and set aside.
4 Heat the remaining oil over moderate heat. Add the celery and stir-fry for 2–3 minutes. Stir the cornflour mixture, then pour over the celery and stir to mix. Return the beef to the wok, increase the heat to high and toss until the ingredients are combined. Add the pineapple and toss until heated through. Season to taste and serve.

Serves 3–4
Preparation time: 35 minutes
Cooking time: 10 minutes

Szechuan Pepper Beef

Szechuan peppercorns, available from spice racks in large supermarkets, are aromatic rather than hot like black or white pepper. They are used extensively in the Szechuan region of China, which is noted for its hot and strongly flavoured cooking. This recipe is typical, combining Szechuan peppercorns with chillies and garlic to create a pungent effect.

- 1 tablespoon Szechuan peppercorns
- 3 tablespoons vegetable oil
- 500 g/1 lb rump or fillet steak, cut into thin strips across the grain
- 1 large red pepper, cored, deseeded and cut lengthways into thin strips
- 2 red chillies, deseeded and finely chopped
- 2.5 cm/1 inch piece fresh root ginger, peeled and cut into matchstick strips
- 2 garlic cloves, crushed

SAUCE:
- 2 teaspoons cornflour
- 4 tablespoons water
- 3 tablespoons soy sauce
- 2 teaspoons dark soft brown sugar

1 First prepare the sauce. Mix the cornflour to a thin paste with the water, then stir in the soy sauce and sugar. Set aside.

2 Heat the wok until hot. Add the Szechuan peppercorns and dry-fry over a gentle heat for 1–2 minutes. Remove from the wok and crush using a mortar and pestle. Set aside.

3 Heat half of the oil in the wok over moderate heat. Add the beef strips and crushed peppercorns, increase the heat to high and stir-fry for 3–4 minutes or until the beef is browned on all sides. Tip the beef and its juices into a bowl and set aside.

4 Heat the remaining oil over moderate heat. Add the red pepper, chillies, ginger and garlic and stir-fry for 2-3 minutes or until softened, taking care not to let the ingredients brown.

5 Return the beef and its juices to the wok and stir to mix with the vegetables. Stir the sauce to mix, then pour over the beef and vegetables. Increase the heat to high and toss until the beef is hot and all the ingredients are evenly combined. Serve at once.

Serves 3–4
Preparation time: 15 minutes
Cooking time: 12 minutes

Beef with Cashew Nuts

- 500 g/1 lb lean fillet steak, thinly sliced into strips
- 2 tablespoons soy sauce
- 1 tablespoon dry sherry
- 3 tablespoons sesame oil
- 3 tablespoons water
- 2 teaspoons cornflour
- salt and pepper
- 1 tablespoon peeled and finely chopped fresh root ginger
- 2 garlic cloves, crushed
- 125 g/4 oz unsalted roasted cashew nuts
- 3 celery sticks, sliced diagonally

1 Place the fillet steak in a bowl and add the soy sauce, sherry, 2 teaspoons of the sesame oil, the water, cornflour, salt and pepper and ginger. Cover and leave to marinate in the refrigerator for at least 20 minutes.

2 Heat the remaining oil in the wok. Remove the strips of steak from the marinade and stir-fry quickly in the hot oil for 2 minutes until brown and sealed on the outside. Remove with a slotted spoon and set aside. Reserve the marinade.

3 Add the garlic, cashew nuts and celery to the wok, and then stir-fry quickly over moderate heat for 2–3 minutes, tossing well.

4 Return the steak to the wok with the reserved marinade and mix well with the nuts and celery. Increase the heat and continue cooking, stirring all the time, until the sauce thickens. Transfer to a serving dish.

Serves 3–4
Preparation time: 10 minutes
Cooking time: 8 minutes

VARIATION

Pork with Cashew Nuts

Substitute 500 g/1 lb pork fillet for the fillet steak. Cut it into thin strips across the grain, then proceed as in the main recipe.

Sliced Pork with Hot Sauce

This recipe is simple and quick to make, relying as it does on chilli sauce for its main flavouring. Take care when using chilli sauce for the first time, because some brands are fiery hot while others are milder and sometimes quite sweet. Do not be surprised to find tomato ketchup in this recipe – it is a common ingredient in Western-influenced Singapore.

- 250 g/8 oz medium egg noodles
- 1 tablespoon sesame oil
- 2 tablespoons vegetable oil
- ½ bunch of spring onions, thinly sliced on the diagonal
- 1–2 garlic cloves, crushed
- 375 g/12 oz pork fillet, cut into thin strips across the grain
- salt

SAUCE:
- 75 ml/3 fl oz tomato ketchup
- about 2 tablespoons hot chilli sauce, to taste
- 150 ml/¼ pint hot water

1 Cook the noodles according to the packet instructions. Drain thoroughly, place in a bowl and sprinkle over the sesame oil. Toss to coat, cover and set aside.

2 To prepare the sauce, put the ketchup in a jug or bowl, add chilli sauce to taste, then stir in the water until evenly mixed. Set aside.

3 Heat the oil in the wok over moderate heat. Add the spring onions and garlic and stir-fry for 1–2 minutes or until softened, taking care not to let them brown.

4 Add the strips of pork, increase the heat to high and stir-fry for 3–4 minutes or until the meat is browned on all sides. Add the sauce and stir until evenly mixed with the pork, then add the noodles and toss until piping hot. Taste the sauce and add more chilli sauce and salt, if necessary. Serve immediately.

Serves 3
Preparation time: 30 minutes
Cooking time: about 8 minutes

Beef in Oyster Sauce

- 2 tablespoons oyster sauce
- 1 tablespoon dry sherry
- 1 tablespoon cornflour
- 250 g/8 oz beef steak, cut into thickish slices
- 125 g/4 oz button mushrooms or 3–4 Chinese dried mushrooms, soaked in warm water for 20 minutes
- 4 tablespoons vegetable oil
- 2 slices fresh root ginger, peeled and chopped
- 2 spring onions, chopped
- 175 g/6 oz broccoli, divided into small florets
- 125 g/4 oz bamboo shoots, sliced
- 1 carrot, sliced
- 1 teaspoon salt
- 1 teaspoon sugar

1 In a bowl, mix together the oyster sauce, sherry and cornflour. Add the beef slices, turn to coat, cover and leave to marinate in the refrigerator for about 20 minutes.
2 If using Chinese dried mushrooms, drain and squeeze dry, discard the stalks and finely slice the caps.
3 Heat half of the oil in the wok. Add the beef and stir-fry for 10–15 seconds. Remove with a slotted spoon and set aside.
4 Heat the remaining oil, then add the ginger and spring onions, mushrooms, broccoli, bamboo shoots and carrot. Add the salt and sugar and stir-fry for 1½ minutes. Add the beef, stir well and moisten with a little stock or water. Heat through and serve at once.

Serves 4
Preparation time: 15 minutes
Cooking time: 5 minutes

VARIATION
Beef in Black Bean Sauce

Soak 3 teaspoons salted black beans in 3 tablespoons water for 20 minutes. Heat 2½ tablespoons vegetable oil in the wok, add 500 g/1 lb beef steak, cut into 2.5 cm/1 inch slices, and stir-fry for 1 minute. Lift out with a slotted spoon and drain on kitchen paper. Mash the beans and their soaking water in the wok, and stir in ½ teaspoon chilli sauce and 2 red peppers, cored, deseeded and cut into 2.5 cm/1 inch squares. Stir in the beef. Blend 1 tablespoon cornflour with 3 tablespoons beef stock and stir into the wok to thicken the sauce. Add 1 tablespoon Chinese rice wine or sherry and stir-fry until the sauce has thickened.

Pork in Black Bean Sauce

- 1 tablespoon soy sauce
- 2 tablespoons dry sherry
- 1 tablespoon sugar
- 1 tablespoon plain flour
- 500 g/1 lb pork spare ribs, chopped into small pieces
- 3 tablespoons vegetable oil
- 1 garlic clove, crushed
- 2 spring onions, thinly sliced on the diagonal
- 2 tablespoons black or yellow bean sauce
- 5 tablespoons Clear Stock (see page 35) or water
- 1 small green pepper, cored, deseeded and sliced
- 1 small red pepper, cored, deseeded and sliced

1 Mix together the soy sauce, sherry, sugar and flour in a large bowl. Add the pork spare ribs and leave in a cool place to marinate for 10–15 minutes.
2 Heat the oil in the wok and add the pork spare ribs. Stir-fry for a few minutes until they are golden. Remove with a slotted spoon and drain on kitchen paper.
3 Add the garlic, spring onions and black or yellow bean sauce to the wok and stir well. Add the pork spare ribs with the clear stock or water, and cook, covered, over high heat for 5 minutes. If necessary, add a little more liquid. Replace the lid and cook for a further 5 minutes.
4 Add the sliced green and red peppers and stir well. Cook for 2 minutes and then remove from the heat. Transfer to a warmed platter and serve immediately.

Serves 4
Preparation time: 10 minutes
Cooking time: 15–20 minutes

Orange Glazed Pork

Oranges are native to China but have been known in Europe since late Roman times, when they were introduced by Arab traders. The first oranges were all bitter, like the Seville orange, for the sweet orange did not reach the West until the 1630s.

- thinly pared rind of 1 large orange, cut into matchstick strips
- 3 tablespoons vegetable oil
- 500 g/1 lb pork fillet, sliced thinly across the grain
- 1 onion, finely chopped
- 2.5 cm/1 inch piece fresh root ginger, peeled and finely chopped
- 4 tablespoons orange juice
- 4 tablespoons clear honey
- 2 tablespoons crunchy peanut butter
- 2 tablespoons soy sauce
- ½ teaspoon chilli powder, or to taste
- sprigs of mint, to garnish

1 Blanch the strips of orange rind in boiling water for 1 minute. Drain, rinse under cold water and drain again. Set aside.

2 Heat 2 tablespoons of the oil in the wok over moderate heat. Add the pork strips, increase the heat to high and stir-fry for 3–4 minutes or until lightly coloured on all sides. Tip the pork and its juices into a bowl and set aside.

3 Heat the remaining oil in the wok. Add the onion and ginger and stir-fry for 2–3 minutes or until softened, taking care not to let it brown. Stir in the orange juice, honey, peanut butter, soy sauce and chilli powder, bring to the boil and stir for 1 minute.

4 Return the pork and its juices to the wok, add half of the orange rind and mix well. Toss until all the ingredients are combined and the pork is piping hot. Serve at once, sprinkled with the remaining orange rind and mint sprigs

Serves 3–4
Preparation time: 15 minutes
Cooking time: 10 minutes

Pork and Vegetables

- 2 tablespoons soy sauce
- 1 tablespoon dry sherry
- 2 teaspoons cornflour
- 250 g/8 oz pork fillet, thinly sliced
- 5 tablespoons vegetable oil
- 2 spring onions, cut into 2.5 cm/1 inch lengths
- 1 slice fresh root ginger, peeled and finely chopped
- 125 g/4 oz fresh bean sprouts
- 1 small green pepper, cored, deseeded and sliced
- few cauliflower or broccoli florets
- 2–3 tomatoes, cut into pieces
- 2 carrots, cut into matchsticks
- 50 g/2 oz green beans, trimmed
- 2 teaspoons salt
- 1 tablespoon sugar
- 3 tablespoons clear stock (see right) or water

1 Mix together the soy sauce, sherry and cornflour in a bowl, and add the pork. Stir well until each slice is coated with the mixture.

2 Heat half of the oil in the wok. Add the sliced pork and stir-fry for 1 minute, then remove with a slotted spoon and set aside.

3 Heat the remaining oil and add the spring onions and ginger, followed by the bean sprouts, green pepper, cauliflower or broccoli, tomatoes, carrots, green beans, salt and sugar. Stir-fry for 1–2 minutes and then add the sliced pork. Moisten with a little stock or water if wished and stir-fry quickly until the vegetables are tender but still crisp. Serve immediately with rice.

Serves 3–4
Preparation time: 15 minutes
Cooking time: 8–10 minutes

Clear Stock

Place 1 kg/2 lb chicken pieces and 750 g/1½ lb pork spare ribs in a large saucepan with 50 g/2 oz unpeeled fresh root ginger, cut into chunks, and 4–5 spring onions. Add 2.75 litres/ 5 pints water and bring to the boil. Skim, then reduce the heat slightly and cook, uncovered, for at least 1½–2 hours. Remove from the heat and leave to cool. When cold, skim off the surface fat. Strain the stock and return to a clean saucepan. Add 50 ml/2 fl oz rice wine or dry sherry and return to the boil. Simmer for 5 minutes before using. This stock can be stored in a covered container in the refrigerator for 4–5 days.

Sweet and Sour Pork

- 250 g/8 oz pork, cut into cubes
- 1 teaspoon salt
- 1½ tablespoons brandy
- 1 egg, beaten
- 1 tablespoon cornflour
- vegetable oil for deep-frying
- 125 g/4 oz bamboo shoots, cut into chunks
- 1 green pepper, cored, deseeded and cut into chunks
- 2 spring onions, cut into 2.5 cm/1 inch lengths
- 1 x 425 g/14 oz can pineapple chunks in juice, drained and juice reserved

SAUCE:

- 3 tablespoons vinegar
- 3 tablespoons sugar
- ½ teaspoon salt
- 1 tablespoon tomato purée
- 1 tablespoon soy sauce
- 1 tablespoon cornflour
- 1 teaspoon sesame oil

1 Place the pork in a bowl and sprinkle with the salt and brandy. Leave to marinate in the refrigerator for 15 minutes. Add the beaten egg and cornflour and blend well.

2 Heat the oil in the wok to 180–190°C/350–375°F, or until a cube of bread browns in 30 seconds. Deep-fry the pork for 3 minutes. Remove the wok from the heat but leave the pork in the oil for a further 2 minutes, then remove with a slotted spoon and drain on kitchen paper. Return the wok to the heat and reheat the pork with the bamboo shoots for 2 minutes. Remove and drain on kitchen paper.

3 Pour off the excess oil, leaving 1 tablespoonful in the wok. Add the green pepper and spring onions. Mix all the sauce ingredients with a little canned pineapple juice and add to the wok, stirring until thickened. Add the pork, bamboo shoots and pineapple and serve hot.

Serves 3–4
Preparation time: 15 minutes
Cooking time: 15 minutes

Deep-fried Wontons

- **24 wonton skins**
- **vegetable oil, for deep-frying**

FILLING:

- **125 g/4 oz minced pork**
- **50 g/2 oz cooked, peeled prawns, finely chopped**
- **2 teaspoons finely chopped spring onions**
- **1 tablespoon Chinese rice wine or dry sherry**
- **1 teaspoon sugar**
- **½ teaspoon salt**

SAUCE:

- **1 tablespoon cornflour**
- **4–5 tablespoons water**
- **1 tablespoon tomato purée**
- **1 tablespoon sugar**
- **2 tablespoons vinegar**
- **1 tablespoon soy sauce**
- **1 tablespoon vegetable oil**

1 To make the filling, put the pork, prawns, spring onions, rice wine or sherry, sugar and salt into a bowl and mix well to form a smooth mixture.

2 Working on a lightly floured surface, put 1 teaspoon of the filling on each wonton skin. Fold over from corner to corner, wetting a small part of the skin on the sides immediately around the filling. Press together firmly to seal.

3 Heat the oil in the wok to 180–190°C/350–375°F, or until a cube of bread browns in 30 seconds. Turn down the heat and fry the wontons in batches for 2–3 minutes or until crispy. Remove with a slotted spoon and drain on kitchen paper.

Keep warm in a low oven.

4 Make the sauce. Put the cornflour into a bowl, add the water and mix to a smooth paste. Stir in the tomato purée, sugar, vinegar and soy sauce. Heat the oil in the wok and pour in the sauce mixture. Stir over moderate heat for 3–4 minutes until smooth. Turn the sauce into a bowl and serve immediately with the wontons.

Serves 4–6

Preparation time: 30 minutes
Cooking time: 10 minutes

Fried Pork Balls

- 2 teaspoons chopped fresh coriander stems
- 2 teaspoons black pepper
- 4 garlic cloves, peeled
- pinch of sugar
- 500 g/1 lb minced pork

- 2 tablespoons nam pla (Thai fish sauce)
- flour, for coating
- 4–5 tablespoons vegetable oil

TO GARNISH:
- fresh coriander leaves

1 Put the coriander stems, pepper, garlic and sugar into a mortar or blender and work to a smooth paste.

2 Put the pork and the coriander paste into a food processor or blender and add the nam pla. Process until the mixture is thick and smooth, then transfer to a bowl.

3 Form the mixture into about 20 small balls, approximately 2.5 cm/1 inch in diameter. Roll the pork balls lightly in a little flour.

4 Heat the oil in the wok and add about 5 pork balls. Fry over moderate heat for 2–3 minutes, or until no liquid is released from the pork balls when they are pierced with a knife. Remove from the wok with a slotted spoon and drain on kitchen paper. Keep warm while you fry the remaining pork balls. Serve hot garnished with fresh coriander leaves.

Serves 4
Preparation time: 15 minutes
Cooking time: 12 minutes

Spring Rolls

- 250 g/8 oz plain flour
- pinch of salt
- 1 egg
- 1 tablespoon flour blended with 1 table-spoon water for the paste
- sunflower oil, for deep-frying

FILLING:

- 1 tablespoon sunflower oil
- 250 g/8 oz lean pork, shredded
- 1 garlic clove, crushed
- 2 celery sticks, sliced
- 125 g/4 oz mushrooms, sliced
- 2 spring onions, chopped
- 125 g/4 oz bean sprouts
- 125 g/4 oz cooked, peeled prawns
- 2 tablespoons light soy sauce

1 Sift the flour and salt into a bowl and beat in the egg and about 300 ml/ ½ pint cold water to make a smooth batter. Lightly oil a 20 cm/8 inch frying pan and set it over moderate heat.

2 Pour in sufficient batter to cover the base of the pan. Cook until the underside is pale golden and then turn the pancake over and cook the other side. Repeat until all the batter is used.

3 To make the filling, heat the oil in the wok and then add the pork. Stir-fry for 2–3 minutes until it is evenly browned. Add the garlic and vegetables and stir-fry for 2 minutes. Mix in the prawns and soy sauce, then remove from the heat and allow to cool.

4 Place 2–3 tablespoons of the filling in the centre of each pancake. Fold in the sides and roll up tightly, sealing the edges with a little of the flour and water paste.

5 Heat the oil for deep-frying in the wok to 180–190°C/350–375°F, or until a cube of bread browns in 30 seconds. Deep-fry the spring rolls two at a time until evenly golden. Drain on kitchen paper and serve hot.

Serves 4–6

Preparation time: 35 minutes
Cooking time: 10 minutes

Fried Golden Bags

- **20 wonton wrappers**
- **20 fresh chives, about 10 cm/4 inches long**
- **oil, for deep frying**

FILLING:

- **1 teaspoon crushed garlic**
- **1 teaspoon chopped coriander root or stem**
- **¼ teaspoon pepper**
- **75 g/3 oz canned water chestnuts, chopped**
- **250 g/8 oz lean minced pork**
- **50 g/2 oz raw prawns, peeled and chopped**
- **2 spring onions, chopped**
- **1 fresh green chilli, deseeded and chopped**
- **1 tablespoon dark soy sauce**
- **1 tablespoon nam pla (Thai fish sauce)**

TO SERVE:

- **plum sauce or chilli sauce**

1 Put the garlic, coriander and pepper in a mortar and pound with a pestle until they are roughly blended and form a paste.

2 To make the filling, put all the filling ingredients into a large bowl and mix together until thoroughly combined. You should end up with a thick paste.

3 Spread out the wonton wrappers on a lightly floured surface and divide the pork filling equally among them, putting a spoonful in the centre of each wrapper.

4 Pull up the 4 corners of the wontons into the middle to make little bags and secure them around the middle where the corners of the wonton wrappers are gathered together with the chives. Take care that the chives do not break as you tie them.

5 Heat the oil for deep frying in a wok or deep-fryer. Fry the little bags in batches, a few at a time, until they are crisp and golden brown. Remove and drain on absorbent kitchen paper. Serve very hot with either plum sauce or chilli sauce.

Serves 4–5
Preparation: 25 minutes
Cooking: 5–10 minutes

Lamb in Lettuce Parcels

- 2 tablespoons vegetable oil
- ½ bunch of spring onions, thinly sliced on the diagonal
- 1 green chilli, deseeded and finely chopped
- 2 garlic cloves, crushed
- 5-15 g/¼-½ oz dried shiitake mushrooms, soaked in warm water for 20 minutes
- 250 g/8 oz lamb fillet, cut into thin strips across the grain
- 75 g/3 oz bean sprouts
- 3 tablespoons soy sauce
- pepper
- about 4 tablespoons hoisin sauce
- 8 crisp lettuce leaves
- fresh mint or basil leaves

DIPPING SAUCE:

- 125 ml/4 fl oz soy sauce
- 2 garlic cloves, crushed
- 1 teaspoon caster sugar
- 1 teaspoon lemon juice

1 First make the dipping sauce. Beat all the ingredients together in a small bowl. Set aside.

2 Heat the oil in the wok over moderate heat until hot. Add the spring onions, chilli and garlic and stir-fry for 2–3 minutes to flavour the oil. Remove the flavourings with a slotted spoon and drain on kitchen paper.

3 Drain the mushrooms, squeeze dry and chop roughly. Add the lamb to the wok and increase the heat to high. Stir-fry for 3–4 minutes or until browned on all sides. Add the mushrooms and bean sprouts and stir-fry for 2–3 minutes, then return the spring onion mixture to the wok and add the soy sauce. Stir-fry until all the ingredients are evenly combined, then add pepper to taste.

4 Spoon a little hoisin sauce on to each lettuce leaf, place a few mint or basil leaves on top, then a spoonful of the lamb mixture. Roll up the lettuce around the lamb tucking the ends in. Serve at once, with the dipping sauce handed separately.

Serves 4

Preparation time: 15 minutes
Cooking time: about 12 minutes

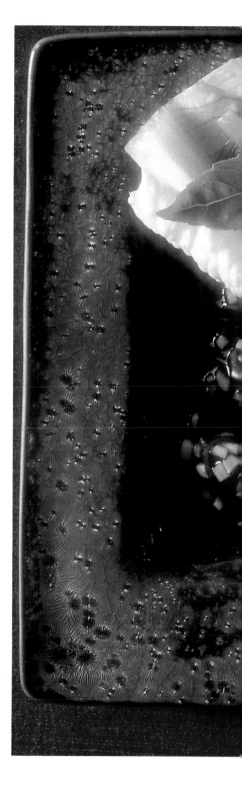

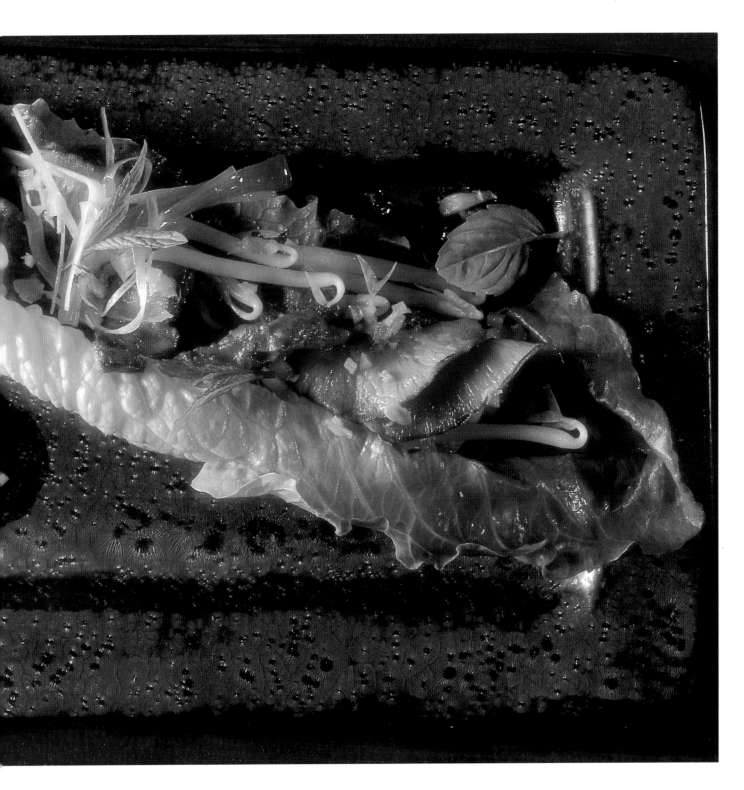

Oriental Lamb

This simple stir-fry is full of crisp, crunchy and colourful vegetables, which make the lamb nutritious and fresh-tasting. You can ring the changes with different vegetables according to the season – there are no hard-and-fast rules. Water chestnuts are available in cans from large supermarkets; they do not have much flavour, but their texture is wonderfully crisp.

- 3 tablespoons vegetable oil
- 500 g/1 lb lamb fillet, cut into thin strips across the grain
- 3 spring onions, thinly sliced on the diagonal
- 1 garlic clove, crushed
- 1 small red pepper, cored, deseeded and cut lengthways into thin strips
- 1 small yellow pepper, cored, deseeded and cut lengthways into strips
- 2 medium courgettes, thinly sliced on the diagonal
- 1 x 225 g (7½ oz) can water chestnuts, drained and thinly sliced
- pepper

SAUCE:
- 2 teaspoons cornflour
- 4 tablespoons water
- 2 tablespoons soy sauce

1 First prepare the sauce. Mix the cornflour to a thin paste with the water, then stir in the soy sauce. Cover and set aside.

2 Heat 2 tablespoons of the oil in the wok. Add the lamb strips, increase the heat to high and stir-fry for 3–4 minutes or until the lamb is browned on all sides. Tip the lamb and its juices into a bowl and set aside.

3 Heat the remaining oil over moderate heat. Add the spring onions, garlic and peppers and stir-fry for 3–4 minutes. Add the courgettes and stir-fry for a further 2 minutes.

4 Return the lamb and its juices to the wok, then add the water chestnuts. Stir the sauce to mix, pour into the wok and increase the heat to high. Toss for 2–3 minutes or until all the ingredients are combined and the lamb is piping hot. Add pepper to taste and serve at once.

Serves 4
Preparation time: 15 minutes
Cooking time: 15 minutes

Lamb with Okra and Tomatoes

- 250 g/8 oz small okra, trimmed
- 3 tablespoons vegetable oil
- 1 onion, thinly sliced
- 1–2 garlic cloves, crushed
- 2 teaspoons ground coriander
- 2 teaspoons turmeric
- 1 teaspoon hot chilli powder, or to taste
- 500 g/1 lb lamb fillet, cut into thin strips across the grain
- 250 g/8 oz ripe tomatoes, skinned and roughly chopped
- finely grated rind and juice of ½ lemon
- ½ teaspoon caster sugar
- salt

1 Blanch the okra in boiling salted water for 5 minutes, then drain, rinse under cold running water and drain again. Set aside.

2 Heat the oil in the wok over moderate heat. Add the onion, garlic, coriander, turmeric and chilli powder and stir-fry for 2–3 minutes or until the onion is softened, taking care not to let the onion brown.

3 Add the lamb strips to the wok, increase the heat to high and stir-fry for 3–4 minutes or until the lamb is browned on all sides.

4 Add the tomatoes and stir-fry until the juices run, then add the lemon rind and juice, sugar, and salt to taste. Stir-fry to mix, then add the okra and toss for 3–4 minutes or until heated through. Serve hot.

Serves 3–4
Preparation time: 15 minutes
Cooking time: about 12 minutes

Fish and Seafood

Rapid-fried Prawns

vegetable oil, for deep-frying

500 g/1 lb raw prawns, peeled and deveined but with tails left on

2 teaspoons cornflour

1 tablespoon cold water

SWEET AND SOUR SAUCE:

2 tablespoons dry sherry

2 tablespoons soy sauce

2 tablespoons vinegar

1 tablespoon sugar

1 teaspoon finely chopped spring onion

1 teaspoon finely chopped fresh root ginger

1 Heat the oil in the wok to 180–190°C/350–375°F, or until a cube of bread browns in 30 seconds. Add the prawns and deep-fry until they turn bright pink. Lift them out with a slotted spoon and drain on kitchen paper.

2 Pour off all but 1 tablespoon of oil from the wok, and increase the heat to high. Quickly mix together the dry sherry, soy sauce, vinegar, sugar, spring onion and ginger in a bowl and add to the wok with the prawns. Cook for about 1 minute, stirring.

3 Mix the cornflour to a smooth paste with the water. Add to the wok and stir until all the prawns are coated with the sauce.

Serves 4

Preparation time: 10 minutes

Cooking time: 5 minutes

Sesame Prawns

You will need large raw prawns for this dish which makes a tasty starter for a dinner party. Splitting and pressing the prawns before cooking is not absolutely essential, but it does help prevent them shrivelling up during deep-frying and adds to the. appearance of the finished dish.

- 12 raw king or tiger prawns, peeled and deveined but with tails left on
- 2 tablespoons plain flour
- 1 large egg
- 2 tablespoons sesame seeds
- salt and pepper
- about 600 ml/1 pint vegetable oil for deep-frying
- flat leaf parsley, to garnish
- soy sauce, for dipping

1 Rinse the prawns under cold running water, then pat dry thoroughly. With a sharp pointed knife, slit the prawns along their undersides. Open them out carefully, place cut-side down on a board and press firmly to flatten them slightly.

2 Sprinkle the flour on a work surface or plate, add the prawns and turn to coat in the flour. Beat the egg in a bowl with the sesame seeds and salt and pepper to taste.

3 Pour the oil into the wok and heat to 180–190°C/350–375°F, or until a cube of bread browns in 30 seconds.

4 Holding the prawns by their tails, dip them one at a time into the egg mixture, then immediately drop them into the hot oil. Deep-fry for 1–2 minutes or until crisp and light golden, then lift out with a slotted spoon and place on kitchen paper to drain. Keep hot while deep-frying the remaining prawns in the same way. Serve at once, garnished with flat leaf parsley, with a bowl of soy sauce for dipping.

Makes 12

Preparation time: 30 minutes
Cooking time: about 10 minutes

Prawns with Broccoli

- 250 g/8 oz cooked king prawns, peeled and deveined
- 1 slice fresh root ginger, peeled and finely chopped
- 1 tablespoon medium or dry sherry
- 1 egg white
- 1 teaspoon cornflour
- 3 tablespoons vegetable oil
- 2 spring onions, finely chopped
- 250 g/8 oz broccoli, divided into small florets and stems trimmed and sliced
- 1 teaspoon salt
- 1 teaspoon sugar

1 Split each prawn in half lengthways and then cut into pieces.

2 Put the prawn pieces into a small bowl with the ginger, sherry, egg white and cornflour. Stir well and then leave in the refrigerator to marinate for about 20 minutes.

3 Heat 1 tablespoon of the oil in the wok and add the prawns. Stir-fry over moderate heat for about 30 seconds. Remove from the wok with a slotted spoon and set aside.

4 Heat the remaining oil in the wok. Add the spring onions and broccoli and stir well. Add the salt and sugar and stir-fry until the broccoli is just tender. Return the prawns to the wok and stir to mix with the broccoli. Serve immediately.

Serves 2–3

Preparation time: 10 minutes
Cooking time: 5 minutes

Prawn Curry

Galangal comes from the same family as ginger. Ground galangal is also sold under the name of laos powder.

- 750 ml/1¼ pints coconut milk (see page 7)
- 2 tablespoons green curry paste (see page 7)
- 2 teaspoons ground galangal
- 750 g/1½ lb raw prawns, peeled and deveined
- 2 tablespoons nam pla (Thai fish sauce)

TO GARNISH:

- 1 tablespoon fresh green chilli, cut into 2.5 cm/1 inch strips
- 4 fresh basil leaves

1 Put the coconut milk into a jug and chill in the refrigerator for at least 1 hour, or until the thick milk rises to the surface. Scoop 250 ml/8 fl oz off the top and put into the wok. Reserve the remaining coconut milk.

2 Bring the coconut milk to the boil, then lower the heat and simmer, uncovered, stirring occasionally, until the coconut oil bubbles to the surface and the liquid has reduced to a quarter of its original volume. Add the green curry paste and galangal and bring the mixture to the boil. Cook over medium to high heat until most of the liquid has evaporated.

3 Rinse the prawns under cold running water. Pat dry on kitchen paper and add to the mixture in the wok. Stir-fry for 3–4 minutes until they are firm and pink.

4 Stir in the remaining coconut milk and nam pla and simmer for 6–8 minutes, stirring occasionally. Serve garnished with strips of green chilli and basil leaves.

Serves 4–6

Preparation time: 10 minutes, plus 1 hour chilling
Cooking time: 30–35 minutes

Prawns in Coconut Sauce

- 16 large raw prawns, peeled and deveined
- 2 tablespoons vegetable oil
- 1 large onion, finely chopped
- 2 stalks lemon grass, chopped
- 2 fresh red chillies, deseeded and sliced
- 2.5 cm/1 inch piece fresh root ginger, shredded
- 1 tablespoon ground cumin
- 1 tablespoon ground coriander
- 2 tablespoons nam pla (Thai fish sauce)
- 250 ml/8 fl oz thick coconut milk (see page 7)
- 3 tablespoons roasted peanuts, coarsely ground
- 2 tomatoes, skinned and chopped
- 1 teaspoon sugar
- juice of ½ lime
- fresh coriander leaves, chopped

1 Rinse the prawns under cold running water, then pat dry on kitchen paper. With a sharp pointed knife, slit along the undersides from head to tail.

2 Heat the oil in the wok. Add the onion and fry until soft and golden. Add the lemon grass, red chillies, ginger, cumin and coriander, and stir-fry for 2 minutes.

3 Add the nam pla and coconut milk to the wok. Stir well and then add the peanuts and chopped tomatoes. Cook gently over low heat until the tomato is soft and the flavours of the sauce are well developed.

4 Stir in the prawns and simmer gently for 5 minutes, or until the prawns are pink and tender. Stir in the sugar, then transfer to a serving dish. To serve, sprinkle with lime juice and coriander.

Serves 4
Preparation time: 20 minutes
Cooking time: 17–20 minutes

Sauté of Scallops with Mangetout

Frozen shelled scallops are available at most good fishmongers, and at the fresh fish counters of many large supermarkets. They are expensive, but quite rich in flavour, so you do not need a large quantity. This recipe allows 4 scallops per person, but you could increase this to 5–6 if you feel 4 is not enough and want to give your guests a special treat.

- 8 shelled scallops with coral, defrosted and dried thoroughly, if frozen
- 3 tablespoons vegetable oil
- 6 spring onions, thinly sliced on the diagonal
- 2.5 cm/1 inch piece fresh root ginger, peeled and finely chopped
- 175 g/6 oz mangetout, trimmed
- 1 garlic clove, crushed
- 1 tablespoon sesame oil
- 2 tablespoons soy sauce
- ½ teaspoon caster sugar
- pepper
- spring onions, to garnish

1 Slice the scallops thickly, detaching the corals and keeping them whole. Set the corals aside.

2 Heat 2 tablespoons of the vegetable oil in the wok over moderate heat. Add the spring onions and ginger and stir-fry for a few seconds. Add the mangetout and garlic and stir-fry for 2 minutes, then tip the vegetable mixture into a bowl and set aside.

3. Heat the remaining vegetable oil with the sesame oil over moderate heat. Add the sliced scallops and stir-fry for 3 minutes. Return the spring onion, ginger and mangetout mixture to the wok, add the reserved corals, soy sauce and sugar and increase the heat to high. Toss for 1–2 minutes or until all the ingredients are combined and piping hot. Season with pepper to taste and serve immediately, garnished with spring onions.

Serves 2
Preparation time: 15 minutes
Cooking time: about 10 minutes

Squid and Green Peppers

- vegetable oil, for deep-frying
- 250 g/8 oz prepared squid, thinly sliced
- 1 green pepper, cored, deseeded and sliced
- 2 slices fresh root ginger, peeled and thinly shredded
- 1 teaspoon salt
- 1 tablespoon soy sauce
- 1 teaspoon vinegar
- pepper
- 1 teaspoon sesame oil

1 Heat the oil in the wok to 180–190°C/ 350–375°F, or until a cube of bread browns in 30 seconds. Add the squid and deep-fry for about 30 seconds, then remove with a slotted spoon and drain on kitchen paper. Carefully pour off the excess oil, leaving about 1 tablespoon of oil in the wok.
2 Return the squid to the wok and add the green pepper and ginger. Stir-fry for a few seconds, then stir in the salt, soy sauce, vinegar and pepper. Cook for about 1 minute, and then add the sesame oil and serve.

Serves 2–4
Preparation time: 15 minutes
Cooking time: 5 minutes

Stir-fried Prawns

- 4 tablespoons vegetable oil
- 3 slices fresh root ginger, peeled
- 2 tablespoons cornflour plus 1 teaspoon
- 1 teaspoon salt
- 1 tablespoon dry sherry
- 1 egg white
- 500 g/1 lb large raw prawns, peeled and deveined but with tails left on
- 2 garlic cloves, crushed
- 2 teaspoons black beans, soaked for 1 hour and drained
- 250 g/8 oz mangetout, trimmed and halved
- 6 water chestnuts, thinly sliced
- ½ tablespoon soy sauce
- 2 tablespoons chicken stock
- 1 teaspoon sesame oil
- shredded spring onions and sprigs of coriander, to garnish

1 Heat the oil in the wok until it starts to smoke. Add the slices of ginger and fry for 30 seconds to flavour the oil. Remove and discard the ginger.

2 In a bowl, mix together 2 tablespoons of the cornflour with the salt, sherry and egg white. Turn the prawns in the mixture until well covered. Add the prawns to the hot oil and stir-fry until they change colour. Remove with a slotted spoon and set aside.

3 Add the garlic, black beans, mangetout and water chestnuts to the wok and stir-fry for 1–2 minutes. Return the prawns to the wok. Mix the remaining cornflour with the soy sauce and the chicken stock and stir into the prawn mixture until thickened. Add the sesame oil and toss well. Serve immediately, garnished with spring onions and coriander sprigs.

Serves 3–4
Preparation time: 10 minutes
Cooking time: 8–10 minutes

VARIATION

Rapid-fried Chilli Prawns

Heat 4 tablespoons of oil in the wok add 1 finely chopped onion, 2 garlic cloves and 1–2 teaspoons chilli powder and fry for 2–3 minutes until softened. Add 500 g/1 lb large raw prawns and stir-fry until they change colour. Add 8 cherry tomatoes, 3 tablespoons tomato purée, 1 tablespoon red wine vinegar, a pinch of sugar and ½ teaspoon salt and stir-fry over high heat until the mixture is thick.

Singapore Crab

When you buy the crab, ask the fishmonger to remove and discard the inedible parts of the crab for you.

- 2 tablespoons vegetable oil
- 2.5 cm/1 inch piece fresh root ginger, peeled and finely chopped
- 1 garlic clove, peeled and finely chopped
- 1 teaspoon hot chilli powder
- 6 tablespoons tomato ketchup
- 2 tablespoons red wine vinegar
- 1 tablespoon soft brown sugar
- 150 ml/¼ pint boiling fish stock
- 1 large cooked crab, chopped into serving pieces with claws and legs cracked open
- salt

TO SERVE:
- cucumber curls or slices
- prawn crackers
- boiled rice

1 Heat the oil in the wok over moderate heat. Add the ginger and garlic and stir-fry for 2–3 minutes until softened, taking care not to let them brown.
2 Add the chilli powder and stir well to combine, then add the ketchup, vinegar and sugar and bring to the boil. Add the boiling fish stock, then the pieces of crab. Stir-fry for about 5 minutes or until the crab is heated through, then add salt to taste.
3 Serve hot, with cucumber curls, prawn crackers and boiled rice handed separately.

Serves 4
Preparation time: about 30 minutes
Cooking time: about 10 minutes

Crab Rolls

- vegetable oil, for deep-frying
- 1 tablespoon plain flour
- 1 tablespoon water

WRAPPING:

- 4 tablespoons plain flour
- ½ teaspoon salt
- 4 tablespoons water
- 4 eggs, beaten

FILLING:

- 2 tablespoons vegetable oil
- 1 egg, beaten
- 1 spring onion, shredded
- 300 g/10 oz crabmeat, flaked
- 1 tablespoon dry sherry
- salt and pepper
- 1 tablespoon cornflour
- 3 tablespoons water

1 To make the wrapping, sift the flour and salt into a bowl, then gradually beat in the water and eggs to form a smooth batter. Place a small lightly oiled frying pan over moderate heat and pour in 4 tablespoons of batter, rotating it until the base is covered. Cook until the edges curl then flip over and cook the other side. Cook all the pancakes in this way.

2 To make the filling, heat the oil in the wok. Add the egg, spring onion and crabmeat. Stir-fry for a few seconds, then add the sherry and salt and pepper. Blend the cornflour with the water and add to the pan, stirring until thickened. Remove from the heat and cool.

3 Blend the flour with the water to make a paste. Place 2 tablespoons of the filling on half of each pancake. Fold over the other half and then fold the right side in towards the left, and the left side in towards the right. Roll up and seal with the flour paste.

4 Heat the oil to 180–190°C/ 350–375°F or until a cube of bread browns in 30 seconds, and deep-fry the crab rolls, a few at a time, until golden brown all over. Drain on kitchen paper and cut into pieces diagonally. Serve immediately.

Serves 6–8
Preparation time: 30 minutes
Cooking time: 10 minutes

Ginger and Spring Onion Crab

- 2 tablespoons sherry
- 1 tablespoon clear stock (see page 35) or water
- 2 tablespoons cornflour
- 1 large crab, chopped into serving pieces, with claws and legs cracked open
- 3 tablespoons vegetable oil
- 4 slices fresh root ginger, peeled and finely chopped
- 4 spring onions, finely chopped
- 1 teaspoon salt
- 1 tablespoon soy sauce
- 2 teaspoons sugar

1 Mix 1 tablespoon of the sherry with the stock or water and cornflour. Pour over the crab and leave to marinate for a few minutes.

2 Heat the oil in the wok until it is very hot. Add the crab and fry briskly for about 1 minute, turning the pieces in the oil.

3 Add the ginger, spring onions, salt, soy sauce, sugar and the remaining sherry. Cook for about 5 minutes, stirring all the time. Add a little water if the mixture becomes very dry. Serve immediately.

Serves 2–4
Preparation time: 20 minutes
Cooking time: 8–10 minutes

Seafood in Batter

- 2 teaspoons garlic mixture (see page 7)
- 2 teaspoons nam pla (Thai fish sauce)
- 500 g/1 lb seafood, e.g. raw prawns, peeled and deveined, and squid cut in rings
- vegetable oil, for deep-frying

TEMPURA BATTER:

- 1 egg
- 150 ml/¼ pint cold water
- 125 g/4 oz self-raising flour
- 2 tablespoons cornflour
- 1 teaspoon baking powder

TO SERVE:

- ready-made shrimp dipping sauce

1 Combine the garlic mixture and nam pla in a shallow bowl. Add the seafood to the pan and turn gently in the garlic marinade. Leave for 5 minutes.

2 Make the tempura batter. Lightly beat together the egg and water in a small bowl. Stir in the flour, cornflour and the baking powder. Do not over-mix; the batter should have a slightly lumpy texture.

3 Remove the prawns and squid from the garlic marinade and dip quickly into the prepared tempura batter. Set aside while you heat the oil ready for frying.

4 Heat the oil for deep-frying in the wok to 180–190°C/350–375°F, or until a cube of bread browns in 30 seconds. Fry the pieces of battered seafood, a few at a time, until puffed up and golden. Remove with a slotted spoon and drain on kitchen paper. Serve with shrimp dipping sauce.

Serves 4

Preparation time: 25 minutes
Cooking time: 5–10 minutes

Seafood with Vegetables

- 125–175 g/4–6 oz raw prawns, peeled and deveined
- 4–6 fresh scallops, sliced
- 1 egg white
- 1 tablespoon cornflour
- vegetable oil, for deep-frying
- 3 celery sticks, sliced
- 1 red pepper, cored, deseeded and sliced
- 1–2 carrots, sliced
- 2 slices fresh root ginger, peeled and shredded
- 2–3 spring onions, chopped
- 2 tablespoons sherry
- 1 tablespoon light soy sauce
- 2 teaspoons chilli bean paste (optional)
- 1 teaspoon salt
- 1 teaspoon sesame oil

1 Leave the prawns whole if small, or cut into 2–3 pieces if large. Put the seafood in a bowl with the egg white and half of the cornflour and mix well.
2 Heat the oil in the wok to 180–190°C/350–375°F, or until a cube of bread browns in 30 seconds. Deep-fry the scallops and prawns for 1 minute, stirring all the time to keep the pieces separate. Remove with a slotted spoon and drain on kitchen paper.
3 Pour off all but 2 tablespoons of oil from the wok. Increase the heat to high and add the vegetables, ginger and spring onions. Stir-fry for about 1 minute. Add the scallops and prawns and stir in the sherry, soy sauce, chilli bean paste, if using, and salt.
4 Mix the remaining cornflour to a smooth paste with a little water, and then add to the wok. Stir well until thickened. Sprinkle with the sesame oil and serve immediately.

Serves 3–4
Preparation time: 20 minutes
Cooking time: 5 minutes

Spicy Fishcakes

- 500 g/1 lb cod fillet, skinned and cut into chunks
- 3 tablespoons red curry paste (see page 7)
- 1 egg
- 3 tablespoons nam pla (Thai fish sauce)
- 1–2 tablespoons rice flour
- 90 g/3 oz green beans, finely chopped
- 1 tablespoon finely shredded kaffir lime leaves
- vegetable oil, for deep frying

TO SERVE:

- sprigs of coriander
- chilli sauce

1 Put the chunks of cod fillet and the red curry paste in a food processor or blender. Process until the fish is worked to a paste. Alternatively, use a pestle and mortar.

2 Transfer the fish mixture to a bowl and add the egg, nam pla and sufficient flour to knead with your hands into a stiff mixture. Work in the beans and lime leaves with your hands.

3 Form the fish mixture into 16–20 balls, then, using your hands, flatten each ball into a round, about 1 cm/ ½ inch thick.

4 Heat the oil in the wok and fry the fishcakes, a few at a time, for 4 minutes on each side, until they are cooked and golden. Take care not to overcook them. Drain on kitchen paper and serve hot, garnished with coriander sprigs and with chilli sauce.

Serves 4–5

Preparation time: 20 minutes
Cooking time: 8–10 minutes

Sweet and Sour Red-Cooked Fish

- 1 x 1 kg/2 lb whole fish, e.g. carp, bream or mullet, cleansed and scaled
- 1 teaspoon salt
- 2 tablespoons flour
- vegetable oil, for deep-frying
- 3 tablespoons vegetable oil
- 15 g/½ oz dried Chinese mushrooms, cooked in warm water for 20 minutes
- 50 g/2 oz bamboo shoots, diced
- 3 garlic cloves, crushed
- 4 spring onions, shredded
- 3 slices fresh root ginger, peeled and shredded
- 25 g/1 oz water chestnuts, sliced

SWEET AND SOUR SAUCE:

- 1 tablespoon cornflour
- 2 tablespoons light soy sauce
- 2 tablespoons sherry
- 1 tablespoon brown sugar
- 1 tablespoon vinegar
- 1 tablespoon tomato purée
- 4 tablespoons stock

1 Wash the fish and dry with kitchen paper. Using a sharp knife, slash both sides of the fish diagonally at 2 cm/ ¼ inch intervals. Sprinkle with salt and dredge with flour.

2 Heat the oil to 180–190°C/ 350–375°F, or until a cube of bread browns in 30 seconds. Deep-fry the whole fish for 6–8 minutes until cooked and crisp, turning the fish halfway through cooking to cook both sides. Remove, drain on kitchen paper and keep warm.

3 Pour off the oil and wipe out the wok with kitchen paper. Heat the vegetable oil in the wok. Drain the mushrooms, squeeze dry and discard the stems. Add the mushroom caps, bamboo shoots, garlic, spring onions and water chestnuts to the wok. Stir-fry briskly for 3–4 minutes.

4 Mix together all the sauce ingredients in a bowl and then stir into the vegetable mixture in the wok. Keep stirring over moderate heat until the sauce has thickened. Arrange the fish on a serving dish and pour the sauce over the top. Serve immediately.

Serves 4

Preparation time: 15 minutes
Cooking time: 15 minutes

Lemon Fried Fish with Mushrooms and Mangetout

Monkfish has a wonderful flavour similar to lobster and its firm texture makes it ideal for stir-frying as it keeps its shape so well. In this recipe, button mushrooms and mangetout are used to help 'stretch' the monkfish and keep the cost down – although cheaper than lobster, monkfish is still an expensive fish.

- 375 g/12 oz monkfish tails, skinned and cut into bite-sized pieces
- 2 tablespoons vegetable oil
- 2 tablespoons sesame oil
- 250 g/8 oz button mushrooms, sliced
- 250 g/8 oz mangetout, trimmed
- sprigs of flat leaf parsley, to garnish

MARINADE:

- 2.5 cm/1 inch piece fresh root ginger, peeled and finely chopped
- 1 garlic clove, crushed
- 3 tablespoons soy sauce
- finely grated rind and juice of 1 large lemon
- ½ teaspoon five-spice powder

1 First make the marinade. Put the ginger and garlic into a shallow dish with the soy sauce, lemon rind and juice and five-spice powder. Add the fish pieces and turn to coat. Cover and leave to marinate for about 30 minutes, turning the fish occasionally.
2 Heat 1 tablespoon each of vegetable and sesame oil in the wok over moderate heat. Add the mushrooms and mangetout and stir-fry for 3–4 minutes or until the juices run from the mushrooms. Tip into a bowl and set aside.
3 Add the remaining oils and heat until hot. Remove the monkfish with a slotted spoon, reserving the marinade, and place in the wok. Stir-fry for 5 minutes, then return the mushrooms and mangetout to the wok with their juices and pour in the marinade. Increase the heat to high and toss until all the ingredients are combined and piping hot. Serve at once, garnished with sprigs of flat leaf parsley.

Serves 3–4
Preparation time: about 40 minutes
Cooking time: about 12 minutes

Vegetable Dishes

Spicy Vegetables

1.2 litres/2 pints water

200 g/7 oz transparent cellophane noodles

8 dried shiitake mushrooms, soaked in warm water for 20 minutes

3 tablespoons sunflower oil

250 g/8 oz Chinese cabbage or Chinese leaves, shredded

pinch of salt

1 large carrot, thinly sliced

125 g/4 oz fresh spinach, cooked and chopped

SAUCE:

1 tablespoon sesame oil

1 tablespoon soy sauce

2 teaspoons sugar

2 teaspoons sesame seeds

½ teaspoon salt

1 Pour the water into a large saucepan and bring to the boil. Add the cellophane noodles, bring back to the boil and boil rapidly for 3 minutes. Remove the noodles from the pan, drain well and set aside.

2 Drain the mushrooms and gently squeeze them dry. Discard the hard stalks and reserve the caps.

3 Heat 2 tablespoons of the oil in the wok and add the cabbage and salt. Stir-fry for 2 minutes, and then remove. Heat the remaining oil in the wok and stir-fry the carrot for 1 minute. Return the cabbage to the wok with the spinach and mushrooms and stir-fry for 2 minutes.

4 To make the sauce, put the sesame oil, soy sauce, sugar, sesame seeds and salt into a saucepan and stir well. Bring gently to the boil then pour over the vegetables in the wok. Add the cellophane noodles and toss well until thoroughly combined. Heat through and serve immediately.

Serves 4
Preparation time: 10 minutes
Cooking time: 15 minutes

Stir-fried Vegetables

- 5–6 Chinese dried mushrooms, soaked in warm water for 20 minutes, or 50 g/2 oz button mushrooms
- 4 tablespoons vegetable oil
- 250 g/8 oz Chinese leaves, thinly sliced
- 175 g/6 oz carrots, thinly sliced on the diagonal
- 125 g/4 oz French beans, trimmed and cut in half
- 1 teaspoon salt
- 1 teaspoon sugar
- 1 tablespoon light soy sauce

1 Drain the mushrooms and squeeze dry. Discard the hard stalks and slice the caps thinly. If using fresh mushrooms just wash and slice them.

2 Heat the oil in the wok until it is smoking. Reduce the heat and add the Chinese leaves and carrots. Stir-fry briskly for 30 seconds.

3 Add the beans and mushrooms and continue stir-frying for 30 seconds. Add the salt and sugar and toss and turn the vegetables until well blended. Stir in the soy sauce and cook for 1 minute. Transfer to a warmed serving dish and serve immediately.

Serves 3–4
Preparation time: 10 minutes
Cooking time: 3–4 minutes

Artichoke and Red Pepper Stir-Fry

Roasted red pepper is soft and sweet, with a smoky 'barbecue' flavour. If you are short of time, omit the roasting of the red pepper, but you will then need to stir-fry the fresh red pepper for a few minutes longer in order to soften it.

- **1 large red pepper**
- **2 tablespoons olive oil**
- **1 onion, finely chopped**
- **2.5 cm/1 inch piece fresh root ginger, peeled and finely chopped**
- **1 garlic clove, crushed**
- **1 x 300 g/10 oz can artichoke hearts, drained and sliced**
- **1 tablespoon balsamic vinegar**
- **salt and pepper**
- **few basil leaves, to garnish**

1 Roast the red pepper under a hot grill, turning it frequently until the skin is charred black on all sides. Wrap in kitchen paper, place immediately in a polythene bag and close tightly. Leave until cold.

2 Unwrap the red pepper and rub off the blackened skin under cold running water. Pull out and discard the core and seeds, then cut the pepper open lengthways, rinse and pat dry with kitchen paper. Cut the pepper lengthways into thin strips, then set aside.

3 Heat the oil in the wok over moderate heat. Add the onion, ginger and garlic and stir-fry for 2–3 minutes or until softened, taking care not to let it brown. Add the artichokes and pepper strips, increase the heat to high and toss until piping hot. Sprinkle over the balsamic vinegar and add salt and pepper to taste. Serve at once, garnished with the basil leaves.

Serves 4
Preparation time: about 30 minutes
Cooking time: about 5 minutes

Chinese Braised Vegetables

- 5–6 Chinese dried mushrooms, soaked in warm water for 20 minutes
- 250 g/8 oz firm bean curd, cut into cubes
- salt
- 4 tablespoons vegetable oil
- 125 g/4 oz carrots, sliced
- 125 g/4 oz mangetout, trimmed
- 125 g/4 oz Chinese leaves, shredded
- 2 spring onions cut into 1.25 cm/½ inch lengths
- 125 g/4 oz bamboo shoots, sliced
- 1 teaspoon sugar
- 1 tablespoon light soy sauce
- 1 teaspoon cornflour
- 1 tablespoon cold water
- 1 teaspoon sesame oil

1 Drain the dried mushrooms and squeeze them dry. Discard the hard stalks and cut the caps into thin slices.

2 Bring a saucepan of lightly salted water to the boil and add the bean curd. Boil for 2–3 minutes until firm. Remove the bean curd pieces with a slotted spoon and drain well on kitchen paper.

3 Heat about half of the oil in the wok. Add the bean curd and fry until lightly browned on both sides. Remove with a slotted spoon and set aside. Heat the remaining oil in the wok. Add the vegetables and stir-fry for 2 minutes. Stir in the bean curd with 1 teaspoon salt, the sugar and soy sauce. Cover, reduce the heat and braise for 3 minutes.

4 Meanwhile, mix the cornflour to a smooth paste with the water. Stir into the braised vegetables in the wok. Increase the heat and continue stirring until the sauce thickens. Sprinkle in the sesame oil and serve immediately.

Serves 4
Preparation time: 20 minutes
Cooking time: 15 minutes

VARIATION

Chinese Braised Bamboo Shoots

Heat 3 tablespoons of oil in the wok, add 1 x 425 g/14 oz can bamboo shoots, drained and sliced into thin strips, and stir-fry until golden. Add 1 tablespoon dry sherry, 2 tablespoons soy sauce, 1 tablespoon sugar, stirring constantly, then add 3 tablespoons boiling water and simmer for 7–8 minutes until all the liquid has evaporated. Stir in 1 tablespoon sesame seed oil and serve hot.

Stir-fried Mixed Vegetables

- 3 tablespoons vegetable oil
- 1 garlic clove, crushed
- 125 g/4 oz cabbage, shredded
- 125 g/4 oz cauliflower, divided into florets
- 125 g/4 oz broccoli, divided into florets
- ½ teaspoon pepper
- 2 tablespoons oyster sauce
- 150 ml/¼ pint chicken or vegetable stock
- 2 carrots, cut into matchstick strips
- 125 g/4 oz mushrooms, thinly sliced
- 1 onion, sliced
- 50 g/2 oz bean sprouts

1 Heat the oil in the wok. Add the crushed garlic and stir-fry quickly over medium heat until golden. Do not allow it to get too brown.

2 Add the shredded cabbage, cauliflower and broccoli, and a generous grinding of black pepper. Stir in the oyster sauce and the chicken or vegetable stock, and then cook, stirring constantly, for 3 minutes.

3 Add the carrots, mushrooms and onion to the wok together with the bean sprouts. Stir-fry for 2 minutes. Transfer the fried vegetables to a large dish or platter and serve immediately.

Serves 4
Preparation time: 15 minutes
Cooking time: 6–7 minutes

VARIATION

Stir-fried Bean Sprouts and Beans

Wash and drain 500 g/1 lb fresh bean sprouts and trim and halve 250 g/8 oz green beans. Heat 3–4 tablespoons sunflower oil in the wok until smoking, add 1 chopped spring onion to flavour the oil, then the green beans and stir-fry for 2 minutes. Add the bean sprouts and stir-fry for 30 seconds, then add 1 teaspoon sugar and 1 teaspoon salt and stir-fry for 1 minute. Serve hot, sprinkled with sesame oil.

Shanghai Stir-Fry

- 4 tablespoons sweet and sour sauce
- 1 x 225 g/7½ oz can pineapple chunks in natural juice, drained, with 3 tablespoons juice reserved
- 2 tablespoons vegetable oil
- 2 carrots, cut into matchstick strips
- 1 fennel bulb, sliced into very thin strips, with any leaves reserved
- 1 red pepper, cored, deseeded and cut lengthways into thin strips
- 1 green pepper, cored, deseeded and cut lengthways into thin strips
- 125 g/4 oz bean sprouts
- 175 g/6 oz Chinese leaves, shredded
- salt and pepper
- chopped nuts (cashews, macadamias or peanuts), to garnish

1 Dilute the sweet and sour sauce with 3 tablespoons reserved pineapple juice and set aside.

2 Heat the oil in the wok over moderate heat. Add the carrots, fennel and red and green peppers and stir-fry for 3–4 minutes until the vegetables are just beginning to soften.

3 Pour the diluted sweet and sour sauce into the wok, increase the heat to high and stir-fry until the mixture is bubbling. Add the pineapple chunks and bean sprouts and stir-fry for 1 minute or until hot, then add the shredded Chinese leaves and toss for 1 further minute or until all the ingredients are well combined and piping hot. Add salt and pepper to taste and serve immediately, sprinkled with the chopped nuts and any reserved fennel leaves.

Serves 4–6

Preparation time: about 20 minutes

Cooking time: about 8 minutes

Baby Corn and Red Peppers in Sweet and Sour Sauce

Some supermarkets have specialist vegetable sections selling such delights as miniature or 'baby' carrots, corn, cauliflowers and mangetout. Some of these are just perfect left whole for stir-frying, especially if they are blanched briefly beforehand.

- 175 g/6 oz baby carrots, scraped if necessary
- 175 g/6 oz baby corn
- 2 tablespoons vegetable oil
- 1 large red pepper, cored, deseeded and cut lengthways into thin strips
- 1 onion, thinly sliced
- 1 garlic clove, crushed
- 4 tablespoons yellow bean sauce
- 1 tablespoon dry sherry or sherry vinegar
- salt and pepper
- flat leaf parsley, to garnish

1 Blanch the carrots in boiling salted water for 2 minutes. Lift out with a slotted spoon, rinse immediately under cold running water and leave to drain. Repeat with the corn.

2 Heat the oil in the wok over moderate heat. Add the red pepper, onion and garlic and stir-fry for 2–3 minutes or until softened, taking care not to let the vegetables brown. Add the carrots and baby corn, increase the heat to high and stir-fry for 3–4 minutes.

3 Add the yellow bean sauce and sherry or sherry vinegar and stir-fry until the sauce coats the vegetables and is piping hot. Add salt and pepper to taste and serve at once, garnished with flat leaf parsley.

Serves 4
Preparation time: 10 minutes
Cooking time: 12 minutes

Stir-fried Mushrooms

- 50 g/2 oz dried shiitake mushrooms, soaked in warm water for 20 minutes
- 1 tablespoon oil
- 1 teaspoon peeled and finely chopped fresh root ginger
- 2 spring onions, finely chopped
- 1 garlic clove, crushed
- 250 g/8 oz button mushrooms
- 1 x 225 g/7½ oz can straw mushrooms, drained
- 1 teaspoon chilli bean sauce or chilli powder
- 2 teaspoons dry sherry
- 2 teaspoons dark soy sauce
- 1 tablespoon chicken stock
- pinch of sugar
- pinch of salt
- 1 teaspoon sesame oil

1 Drain the mushrooms and squeeze them dry. Discard the hard stalks.
2 Heat the oil in the wok over moderate heat. Add the ginger, spring onions and garlic and stir-fry briskly for 5–10 seconds.
3 Add the dried mushrooms and button mushrooms to the wok and cook for 5 minutes, stirring all the time.
4 Add the straw mushrooms, chilli bean sauce or chilli powder, sherry, soy sauce, chicken stock, sugar, salt and sesame oil. Mix well, then stir-fry for 5 minutes. Serve at once.

Serves 4
Preparation time: 5 minutes
Cooking time: 10 minutes

VARIATION

Garlic Mushrooms

Heat 2 tablespoons of oil with 15 g/½ oz butter in the wok. Add 375 g/12 oz thinly sliced wild mushrooms, 3–4 crushed garlic cloves and season with salt and pepper. Increase the heat to high, add 2–3 tablespoons Chinese rice wine or dry sherry and stir-fry for 4–5 minutes. Stir in 3–4 tablespoons chopped parsley and serve at once.

Crispy Seaweed

Purple seaweed (laver), hair seaweed and broad seaweed are the types of true seaweed most frequently used in Chinese cooking, often in soups in conjunction with other vegetables. To prepare, seaweeds must be soaked in water for at least 20 minutes, but preferably overnight, before use, and should be rinsed thoroughly before and after soaking. This recipe for spring greens, served in restaurants as Crispy Seaweed, has a wonderfully crisp crunchy texture.

- **750 g/1½ lb spring greens, shredded finely**
- **vegetable oil, for deep-frying**
- **1½ teaspoons caster sugar**
- **1 teaspoon salt**

1 Spread out the shredded spring greens on kitchen paper for about 30 minutes until thoroughly dry.

2 Heat the oil in the wok to 180–190°C/350–375°F, or until a cube of bread browns in 30 seconds. Turn off the heat for 30 seconds and then add a small batch of shredded spring greens. Turn up the heat to moderate and deep-fry the greens until they begin to float on the surface of the oil. Take care, as they tend to spit while they are cooking.

3 Remove the greens with a slotted spoon and drain on kitchen paper. Cook the remaining greens in batches in the same way. When they are all cooked, transfer to a bowl and sprinkle over the sugar and salt. Toss gently to mix and serve warm or cold.

Serves 8
Preparation time: 10 minutes
Cooking time: 10 minutes

VARIATION

Stir-fried Lettuce

This recipe intensifies the greenness of the lettuce while retaining the firmness of its texture.

Discard the outer leaves of 1 large cos lettuce and wash the remainder well. Shake off the excess water and tear the larger leaves into 2–3 pieces. Heat 2–3 tablespoons sunflower oil in the wok, add 1 teaspoon salt and the lettuce leaves and stir vigorously. As soon as the leaves begin to wilt, quickly transfer them to a serving dish and serve immediately.

Aubergines in Fragrant Sauce

- vegetable oil for deep-frying
- 250 g/8 oz aubergines, peeled and cut into chip-sized strips
- 2 spring onions, finely chopped
- 1 slice fresh ginger root, peeled and finely chopped
- 1 garlic clove, peeled and finely chopped
- 125 g/4 oz pork fillet, cut into matchstick strips
- 1 tablespoon soy sauce
- 1 tablespoon dry sherry
- 2 teaspoons chilli sauce
- 2 tablespoons cornflour

1 Heat the oil in the wok. Add the aubergine 'chips' and deep-fry for 1–2 minutes until golden. Remove with a slotted spoon and drain on kitchen paper.

2 Carefully pour off the oil to leave only 1 tablespoonful in the wok. Quickly stir-fry the spring onions, ginger and garlic, followed by the pork. Blend in the soy sauce, sherry and chilli sauce, and then add the aubergine 'chips'. Stir-fry for 1–2 minutes.

3 Mix the cornflour with a little water in a small bowl and then stir it into the mixture in the wok. When the sauce thickens, remove from the heat and serve immediately.

Serves 2–3

Preparation time: 15 minutes
Cooking time: 5–7 minutes

Stir-fried Green Beans

- 3 tablespoon vegetable oil
- 2 garlic cloves, crushed
- 2 shallots, thinly sliced
- 1 slice fresh root ginger, peeled and chopped
- 1 fresh red chilli, deseeded and finely chopped
- ½ teaspoon salt
- 500 g/1 lb green beans, trimmed and strings removed and divided into 5 cm/ 2 inch lengths
- 50 g/2 oz unsalted cashew nuts
- 125 ml/4 fl oz chicken stock
- 2 tablespoons dry sherry
- 1 tablespoon light soy sauce
- 1 teaspoon vinegar
- 1 teaspoon sugar
- black pepper

1 Heat the oil in the wok. Add the garlic, shallots and ginger. Stir-fry briskly over moderate heat for 1 minute. Stir in the red chilli and salt and continue stir-frying for 30 seconds.

2 Add the green beans and cashew nuts to the wok and toss well to combine with the garlic, shallots and spices. Stir-fry quickly for 1 minute to brown the cashew nuts.

3 Add the chicken stock, dry sherry, soy sauce, vinegar and sugar to the wok and bring to the boil. Reduce the heat slightly and continue stir-frying for about 4 minutes, stirring and turning, until the beans are cooked and the liquid has thickened. Turn into a warmed serving dish and serve immediately, seasoned with a generous sprinkling of black pepper.

Serves 4
Preparation time: 10 minutes
Cooking time: 7–8 minutes

Noodles and Rice

Crispy Rice Vermicelli

vegetable oil, for deep-frying	50 g/2 oz chicken breast, thinly sliced
150 g/5 oz rice vermicelli	2 tablespoons tamarind water
6 tablespoons vegetable oil	4 tablespoons brown sugar
1 egg, beaten	1 tablespoon salted soya bean flavouring
1 tablespoon sliced shallots	1 tablespoon nam pla (Thai fish sauce)
1 tablespoon sliced garlic	TO GARNISH:
50 g/2 oz raw prawns, peeled and cut in half lengthways	1 fresh red chilli, deseeded and sliced
	2 tablespoons chopped coriander leaves

1 Heat the oil in the wok to 180–190°C/350–375°F. It will be ready when a piece of vermicelli, dropped into the wok, pops open immediately. Deep-fry the vermicelli in batches until it pops and turns a rich creamy colour. Remove with a slotted spoon, drain on kitchen paper and keep warm without covering, or it will become soft.

2 Heat a little of the vegetable oil in a small pan and add the beaten egg, tilting the pan until it covers the base. Remove the omelette when it is set and cooked, and roll up and cut into thin strips. Keep them warm.

3 Heat the remaining oil in the wok and stir-fry the shallots and garlic until tender and golden brown. Remove, drain on kitchen paper and keep warm. Add the prawns and sliced chicken breast to the wok and stir-fry for 5 minutes. Drain off any excess oil.

4 Stir in the tamarind water, sugar, soya bean flavouring and nam pla. Cook for 5 minutes until sticky. Add the vermicelli, shallots and garlic to the wok, mix well and cook over very low heat for 2–3 minutes. Transfer to a serving dish, top with the omelette strips, and serve garnished with sliced chilli and coriander leaves.

Serves 4
Preparation time: 15 minutes
Cooking time: 17–18 minutes

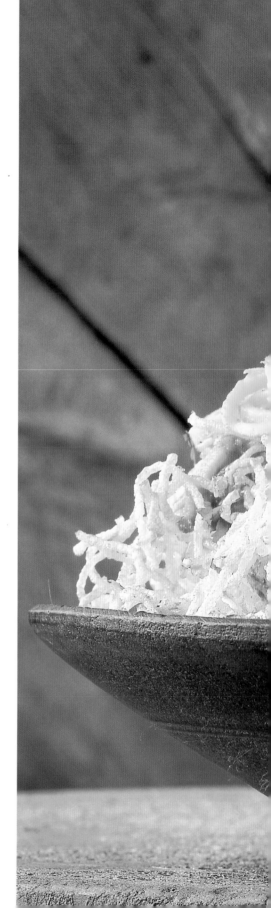

Rice Vermicelli in Coconut Milk

- 250 g/8 oz soaked rice vermicelli
- 2 teaspoons vegetable oil
- 2 eggs, beaten
- 575 ml/18 fl oz coconut milk (see page 7)
- ½ onion, roughly chopped
- 250 g/8 oz raw prawns, shelled
- 4 tablespoons salted soya bean flavouring
- 2 tablespoons sugar
- 2 tablespoons tamarind juice or
  1 tablespoon lemon juice
- 300 g/10 oz bean sprouts
- 125 g/4 oz spring onions, chopped

TO GARNISH:

- 3 tablespoons chopped coriander leaves
- 2 red chillies, deseeded and sliced
- 1 lemon, sliced lengthways

1 Bring a large saucepan of water to the boil, add the soaked rice vermicelli and cook, stirring occasionally, for 15 minutes. Drain well and set aside.
2 Heat the oil in an omelette pan or small frying pan and add the eggs. Tilt the pan to form an omelette, lifting the sides of the omelette to allow any uncooked egg mixture to flow underneath. Remove the cooked, set omelette from the pan and slice into thin shreds. Keep warm.
3 Bring the coconut milk to the boil in the wok. Cook over high heat for 10 minutes until a film of oil forms on top. Stir in the onion, prawns, soya bean flavouring, sugar and tamarind or lemon juice. Cook for 5 minutes, then transfer half of the mixture to a bowl and keep warm.

4 Add the reserved vermicelli to the mixture in the wok. Mix well and cook for 5 minutes. Stir in half of the bean sprouts and spring onions. Pile the vermicelli mixture on to a serving dish and top with the reserved prawn mixture and shredded omelette. Garnish with coriander, chillies and lemon slices, and serve with the remaining bean sprouts and spring onions.

Serves 4
Preparation time: 15 minutes
Cooking time: 45 minutes

Mee Krob

- 150 g/5 oz green beans, cut crossways in half
- about 600 ml/1 pint vegetable oil, for deep-frying, plus 2 tablespoons
- 1 onion, finely chopped
- 2 garlic cloves, crushed
- 2 chicken breasts, boned, skinned and cut into strips across the grain
- 1 teaspoon hot chilli powder, or to taste
- 250 g/8 oz peeled cooked prawns, defrosted and dried thoroughly, if frozen
- 3 tablespoons soy sauce
- 2 tablespoons nam pla (Thai fish sauce)
- 1 tablespoon vinegar
- 2 teaspoons sugar
- 250 g/8 oz rice vermicelli
- salt

TO GARNISH:

- about 50 g/2 oz bean sprouts
- shredded rind of 2 limes or 1 orange
- red chilli flowers (see page 9)
- fresh coriander leaves

1 Blanch the beans in boiling salted water for 2 minutes. Drain, rinse under cold running water and drain again. Set aside.

2 Heat the 2 tablespoons of oil in the wok until hot. Add the onion and garlic and stir-fry for 1–2 minutes until softened without browning.

3 Add the chicken strips, increase the heat and stir-fry for 3–4 minutes or until lightly coloured. Sprinkle over the chilli powder, then add the prawns and stir-fry for 1 minute. Add the soy and fish sauces, the vinegar and sugar and mix well. Tip into a bowl, cover and keep warm.

4 Wipe the wok clean with kitchen paper. Pour in the oil for deep-frying and heat to 180–190°C/350–375°F, or until a cube of bread browns in 30 seconds. Deep-fry the vermicelli a handful at a time, just until they swell and puff up (do not let them colour). Remove with a slotted spoon and drain on kitchen paper. Keep hot while deep-frying the remainder.

5 Quickly pour off all the oil from the wok and wipe clean again. Return the wok to a high heat, add the chicken and prawn mixture and the beans and toss quickly to warm through. Add three-quarters of the vermicelli and toss for a further 30 seconds or so. Transfer to a serving platter. Garnish with the remaining vermicelli and other suggested garnishes and serve.

Serves 4

Preparation time: about 30 minutes
Cooking time: about 20 minutes

Szechuan Noodles

- 350 g/12 oz thin egg noodles
- 250 g/8 oz minced pork
- 2 tablespoons dark soy sauce
- 1 tablespoon dry sherry
- ½ teaspoon salt
- 4 tablespoons peanut or vegetable oil
- 3 garlic cloves, crushed
- 2.5 cm/1 inch piece fresh root ginger, peeled and finely chopped
- 3 spring onions, chopped
- 1–2 fresh red chillies, deseeded and finely chopped
- 1 tablespoon hot soy bean paste
- 1 tablespoon peanut butter
- 175 ml/6 fl oz chicken stock
- pepper
- deseeded, chopped fresh red chilli, to garnish

1 Cook the egg noodles according to packet instructions until tender. Drain well and divide among 4 individual bowls or one large one.

2 Put the minced pork into a bowl with the soy sauce, sherry and salt and mix well to coat the pork thoroughly. Heat the oil in the wok and add the pork. Stir-fry until lightly browned. Remove with a slotted spoon and drain on kitchen paper.

3 Add the garlic, ginger, spring onions and chillies to the wok and stir-fry for 1 minute. Add the hot soy bean paste and peanut butter and stir well over moderate heat for a few seconds.

4 Add the chicken stock, bring to the boil and then simmer for about 5 minutes until thickened. Stir in the pork and continue cooking over low heat for 1 minute. Ladle the sauce over the noodles and sprinkle with plenty of pepper. Garnish with chopped chilli.

Serves 4

Preparation time: 15 minutes
Cooking time: 10 minutes

Noodles with Crab Sauce

- 150 g/5 oz egg noodles
- 2 tablespoons vegetable oil
- 125 g/4 oz spinach or cabbage, roughly chopped
- 125 g/4 oz drained canned crabmeat
- 1 teaspoon soy sauce
- 250 ml/8 fl oz Clear Stock (see page 35)
- 1 spring onion, finely chopped, to garnish

1 Cook the egg noodles according to packet instructions until just tender but still firm. Drain well, then transfer them to a warmed serving dish. Set aside in a warm place while you prepare the sauce.

2 Heat the oil in the wok and add the crabmeat and spinach or cabbage. Stir-fry for 1 minute.

3 Add the soy sauce and stock to the wok and cook briskly for 2–3 minutes, stirring occasionally. Pour the crabmeat sauce over the warm egg noodles and sprinkle with chopped spring onion to garnish. Serve immediately.

Serves 2–3
Preparation time: 10 minutes
Cooking time: 15 minutes

Rice Vermicelli with Seafood Sauce

- vegetable oil, for deep-frying
- 50 g/2 oz rice vermicelli, broken into pieces

SEAFOOD SAUCE:

- 1 tablespoon vegetable oil
- 1 onion, finely chopped
- 2 garlic cloves, crushed
- 250 g/8 oz raw prawns, peeled
- 75 g/3 oz crabmeat

- 2 teaspoons brown sugar
- 2 tablespoons tamarind water (see right)
- 1 teaspoon salt
- 1 tablespoon soy sauce

TO GARNISH:

- 2 teaspoons finely grated orange rind
- 2 red chillies, deseeded and shredded
- chopped coriander leaves
- 125 g/4 oz fresh bean sprouts

1 Heat the oil for deep-frying in the wok to 180–190°C/350–375°F, or until a cube of bread browns in 30 seconds. Fry the rice vermicelli in small batches for about 30 seconds, until the strands swell and puff up. Remove with a slotted spoon and drain on kitchen paper.

2 To make the seafood sauce, heat the oil in the wok. Add the onion and garlic and fry for a few minutes until lightly brown.

3 Add the peeled prawns and crabmeat and cook for 2–3 minutes until the prawns firm up and turn pink. Stir in the brown sugar, tamarind water, salt and soy sauce.

4 Add the fried vermicelli and stir well. Adjust the seasoning if necessary, then heat through gently. Transfer to a warm serving dish and garnish with orange rind, chillies and coriander. Arrange the bean sprouts around the edge of the dish. Serve hot.

Serves 4
Preparation time: 15 minutes
Cooking time: 10 minutes

Tamarind Water

- 25 g/1 oz tamarind
- 150 ml /¼ pint warm water

1 Wash the tamarind and place it in a bowl, pour in the warm water and leave to soak for 5–10 minutes. The longer you leave it, the stronger the flavour of the tamarind water.

2 Squeeze out as much tamarind pulp as possible, then press the thickened liquid through a sieve. Use at once.

3 If you wish to store the tamarind water, strain it into a saucepan and bring to the boil. Remove from the heat and allow to cool in the pan. Transfer to a bowl, cover and store in the refrigerator.

Chow Mein

This dish, which literally translated means "stir-fried noodles", is well known to everyone who eats in Chinese restaurants. Originally invented by Chinese immigrants to the USA, these noodles are now cooked all over the Western world, and with almost any meat, fish or vegetable added to them – there are no hard-and-fast rules for making chow mein.

- 250 g/8 oz Chinese rice noodles
- 2 tablespoons vegetable oil
- 3–4 spring onions, thinly sliced on the diagonal
- 2.5 cm/1 inch piece fresh root ginger, peeled and finely chopped
- 1 garlic clove, crushed
- 2 chicken breasts, boned, skinned and cut into thin strips across the grain
- 125 g/4 oz mangetout, trimmed
- 125 g/4 oz lean sliced cooked ham, shredded
- 75 g/3 oz bean sprouts
- pepper

SAUCE:

- 2 teaspoons cornflour
- 8 tablespoons cold chicken stock or water
- 2 tablespoons soy sauce
- 2 tablespoons rice wine or dry sherry
- 2 teaspoons sesame oil

1 Cook the rice noodles according to packet instructions. Drain the noodles, rinse under cold water and set aside.
2 To prepare the sauce, put the cornflour into a bowl and mix to a paste with 2 tablespoons of the stock or water. Stir in the remaining stock or water, the soy sauce, rice wine or sherry and the sesame oil. Set aside.
3 Heat the oil in the wok over moderate heat. Add the spring onions, ginger and garlic and stir-fry for 1–2 minutes or until softened, taking care not to let them brown. Add the chicken, increase the heat to high and stir-fry for 3–4 minutes or until lightly coloured on all sides.
4 Add the mangetout and stir-fry for 1–2 minutes or until just tender, then add the ham and bean sprouts and stir-fry to combine. Stir the sauce, pour into the wok and bring to the boil, stirring constantly. Add the drained noodles and toss until combined and piping hot. Add pepper to taste and serve at once.

Serves 4

Preparation time: 30 minutes
Cooking time: about 15 minutes

Noodles with Prawn Sauce

- 500 g/1 lb egg noodles
- 75 g/3 oz dried Chinese mushrooms, soaked in warm water for 20 minutes
- 2 tablespoons vegetable oil
- 125 g/6 oz boneless, skinless chicken, diced
- 1 garlic clove, crushed
- 2 slices fresh root ginger, peeled and chopped
- 4 spring onions, cut diagonally into 1 cm/½ inch pieces
- 175 g/6 oz cooked, peeled prawns
- 2 tablespoons soy sauce
- 2 tablespoons dry sherry
- ½ teaspoon salt
- 900 ml/1½ pints clear stock (see page 35)
- 2 tablespoons cornflour
- 50 g/2 oz cooked lean ham, shredded

1 Cook the noodles according to packet instructions until they are just tender. Drain well and divide among 6 bowls. Keep warm.

2 Drain the Chinese mushrooms, reserving the cooking liquid, and squeeze them dry. Discard the stalks and slice the caps thinly.

3 Heat the oil in the wok. Add the chicken, garlic and ginger and stir-fry for 2–3 minutes. Add the spring onions and Chinese mushrooms and stir-fry for 2 minutes.

4 Add the prawns, soy sauce, sherry, salt and clear stock to the wok. Bring to the boil, then simmer over gentle heat for 5 minutes. Mix the cornflour with a little water and stir into the liquid in the wok. Keep stirring over low heat until it thickens slightly. Pour over the noodles, sprinkle with the shredded ham and serve immediately.

Serves 6
Preparation time: 10 minutes
Cooking time: 20 minutes

Fried Noodles with Vegetables

- 4 tablespoons vegetable oil
- 2 garlic cloves, crushed
- 125 g/4 oz medium-sized egg noodles, soaked and drained
- 2 teaspoons dark soy sauce
- 125 g/4 oz mixed sliced chicken breast, prepared squid and cooked, peeled prawns
- ½ teaspoon pepper
- 2 tablespoons nam pla (Thai fish sauce)
- 125 g/4 oz mixed shredded cabbage and broccoli florets
- 300 ml/½ pint chicken stock
- 1 tablespoon cornflour
- 2 tablespoons water
- 1 tablespoon salted soya bean flavouring
- 2 tablespoons sugar

1 Heat half of the oil in the wok. Add half of the garlic and stir-fry for 1 minute until golden brown. Add the noodles and soy sauce and cook, stirring, for 3–5 minutes. Transfer to a serving dish and keep warm.

2 Heat the remaining oil in the wok and add the rest of the garlic. Stir-fry for 1 minute until golden brown. Add the chicken breast, squid and prawn mixture, pepper and nam pla. Stir-fry for 5 minutes.

3 Add the shredded cabbage and broccoli florets to the chicken and seafood mixture in the wok and stir-fry for 3 minutes.

4 Stir the chicken stock into the wok. Mix the cornflour with the water and stir into the wok. Add the soya bean flavouring and sugar and bring to the boil. Lower the heat and cook for 3 minutes, stirring constantly. Pour the thickened sauce over the noodles and serve immediately.

Serves 4
Preparation time: 10 minutes
Cooking time: 20 minutes

Rice Sticks with Beef Sauce

- 500 g/1 lb rice sticks, soaked and drained
- 2 tablespoons dark soy sauce
- 4 tablespoons vegetable oil
- 1 garlic clove, crushed
- 300 g/10 oz minced beef
- ½ tablespoon nam pla (Thai fish sauce)
- ½ tablespoon curry powder
- 1 teaspoon sugar
- ¼ teaspoon pepper
- 1 tablespoon cornflour
- 3 tablespoons light soy sauce
- 1 small onion, chopped
- 1 tomato, skinned and chopped
- 350 ml/12 fl oz chicken stock

TO SERVE:

- 1 lettuce, separated into leaves
- 2 tablespoons chopped coriander leaves

1 Spread out the rice sticks in a large shallow dish. Sprinkle with dark soy sauce and mix thoroughly, using 2 spoons or chopsticks, making sure the rice sticks are well coated.

2 Heat 2 tablespoons of the vegetable oil in the wok and add the rice sticks. Stir-fry for 3–5 minutes, then transfer to a serving dish and keep warm.

3 Heat the remaining oil in the wok, add the garlic and stir-fry for 1 minute or until golden brown. Add the beef, nam pla, curry powder, sugar and pepper and stir well.

4 In a bowl, mix the cornflour to a paste with the light soy sauce. Stir into the beef mixture and cook for 10–15 minutes, stirring frequently, until the beef is cooked and crumbly. Stir in the onion, tomato and stock and bring to the boil. Lower the heat and simmer for 5 minutes.

5 Serve the rice sticks on a bed of lettuce topped with the beef mixture. Garnish with the chopped coriander.

Serves 4–6

Preparation time: 10 minutes
Cooking time: 25 minutes

Thai-style Fried Rice Sticks

- 2 tablespoons vegetable oil
- 1 garlic clove, crushed
- 125 g/4 oz boneless, skinless chicken breast, thinly sliced
- 125 g/4 oz crabmeat
- 125 g/4 oz raw prawns, peeled and deveined
- 125 g/4 oz rice sticks, soaked for 24 hours and drained
- 2 tablespoons nam pla (Thai fish sauce)
- 2 tablespoons sugar
- ½ tablespoon lemon juice
- ¼ teaspoon pepper
- 1 tablespoon ground dried shrimp
- 1 tablespoon chopped preserved turnip
- ½ teaspoon ground chilli
- 2 tablespoons crushed roasted peanuts
- 1 egg
- 2 tablespoons chopped spring onion tops
- 125 g/4 oz bean sprouts

TO SERVE:
- 1 lemon, sliced and quartered

1 Heat the oil in the wok. Add the garlic and stir-fry for 1 minute until golden. Add the chicken, crabmeat and prawns and stir-fry for 3 minutes. Stir in the drained rice sticks, nam pla, sugar, lemon juice and pepper and cook for 1 minute.

2 Add the dried shrimp, preserved turnip, ground chilli and the crushed peanuts, stirring all the time until well mixed.

3 Break the egg into the wok and continue stirring. Add the spring onion tops and bean sprouts, then stir-fry for 3 minutes until the egg is set and the rice sticks are tender. If the rice sticks are hard, add 2 more tablespoons of water and cook until absorbed. Serve garnished with the sliced lemon and bean sprouts.

Serves 4
Preparation time: 15 minutes
Cooking time: 10 minutes

VARIATION

Stir-fried Rice Sticks with Beef and Green Beans

Heat the oil and fry the garlic as for the main recipe. Add 100 g/4 oz thinly sliced fillet steak, season generously with pepper and stir-fry for 4–6 minutes. Add the rice sticks and cook for 3 minutes. Add 100 g/4 oz sliced green beans with 2 teaspoons dark soy sauce, 2 tablespoons nam pla (Thai fish sauce), 2 tablespoons of sugar and 1 beaten egg , mix well and cook for 3 further minutes. Serve immediately.

Special Egg-Fried Rice

- 2–3 eggs
- 2 spring onions, finely chopped
- 2 teaspoons salt
- 3 tablespoons vegetable oil
- 125 g/4 oz cooked peeled prawns
- 125 g/4 oz cooked meat, e.g. chicken or pork, diced
- 50 g/2 oz bamboo shoots, diced
- 4 tablespoons fresh or frozen peas, cooked
- 1 tablespoon light soy sauce
- 375–500 g/12 oz–1 lb cold cooked rice
- chopped spring onions, to garnish

1 Break the eggs into a small bowl and add 1 teaspoon of the finely chopped spring onions and a pinch of the salt. Beat lightly together with a fork to combine them.

2 Heat about 1 tablespoon of the oil in the wok and add the beaten egg mixture. Stir constantly until the eggs are scrambled and set. Remove the scrambled eggs from the wok and set aside in a bowl.

3 Heat the remaining oil in the wok, and add the prawns, meat, bamboo shoots, peas and the remaining chopped spring onions. Stir-fry briskly for 1 minute, and then stir in the soy sauce.

4 Stir-fry for 2–3 minutes and then add the cooked rice, breaking it up, together with the scrambled eggs and the remaining salt. Stir well to break up the scrambled eggs into small pieces and separate the grains of rice.

Serve hot, garnished with spring onions.

Serves 4
Preparation time: 10 minutes
Cooking time: 8–10 minutes

Fried Rice with Pork

- 2 tablespoons vegetable oil
- 1 garlic clove, crushed
- 150 g/5 oz pork fillet, sliced
- 3 tablespoons light soy sauce
- 2 eggs
- 1 tablespoon tomato purée
- 1 tablespoon sugar
- 1 small onion, sliced
- 750 g/1½ lb cooked rice (about 175 g/6 oz raw weight)

TO GARNISH:

- ¼ cucumber, thinly sliced
- 1 lemon, cut into wedges
- 2 tablespoons chopped coriander leaves
- 1 red chilli, deseeded and shredded

1 Heat the oil in the wok. Add the garlic and stir-fry for 1 minute.

2 Add the pork fillet to the wok together with 1 teaspoon of the soy sauce and stir-fry for 5 minutes over moderate heat.

3 Break the eggs into the wok and cook for 2 minutes, stirring vigorously. Add the tomato purée, sugar, the remaining soy sauce and the sliced onion. Stir-fry briskly for 1 minute.

4 Add the rice and continue stir-frying for 5 minutes. Transfer the mixture to a shallow serving dish or 4 plates and garnish with the sliced cucumber, lemon wedges, coriander leaves and shredded red chilli. Serve immediately.

Serves 4

Preparation time: 10–15 minutes
Cooking time: 15 minutes

Nasi Goreng

- 250 g/8 oz long-grain rice
- 750 ml/1¼ pints water
- 2 eggs
- 2½ tablespoons vegetable oil
- 1 small onion, roughly chopped
- 2 garlic cloves, roughly chopped
- 1 fresh green chilli, deseeded and roughly chopped
- 1 cm/½ inch piece terasi (shrimp paste) or 1–2 teaspoons anchovy essence, according to taste
- 1 teaspoon tomato purée
- 250 g/8 oz boneless lean cooked chicken, pork or beef, cut into thin strips
- 250 g/8 oz cooked peeled prawns, defrosted and dried thoroughly, if frozen
- about 3 tablespoons soy sauce
- salt and pepper

TO GARNISH:
- fried onion rings (see page 8)
- sprigs of coriander
- few cucumber slices

1 Rinse the rice under cold running water, then place in a pan. Add the measured water and salt and bring to the boil. Stir once, cover and simmer for 15–20 minutes, or until the water is absorbed. Remove from the heat, turn the rice into a sieve and rinse under cold running water. Set aside.
2 Beat the eggs and season to taste. Heat 1½ teaspoons of the oil in an omelette pan, add the eggs and make an omelette in the usual way. Slide the omelette on to a board and roll up tightly. Set aside. Pound the onion, garlic, chilli and terasi, if using, to a paste using a mortar and pestle, or

work in a food processor until smooth.
3 Heat the remaining oil in the wok over moderate heat. Add the onion mixture with the anchovy essence, if using, and tomato purée and stir-fry for 2–3 minutes, taking care not to let the mixture brown.
4 Add the meat, increase the heat and stir-fry for 1–2 minutes or until hot. Add the prawns and stir-fry for 1 further minute. Tip the cooked rice into the wok and stir-fry for 1–2 minutes or until the rice is mixed with the meat

and prawns, using chopsticks to help separate the grains. Sprinkle over soy sauce to taste.
5 Transfer the nasi goreng to a serving platter. Quickly cut the rolled omelette into thin rings and arrange on top of the nasi goreng. Garnish with prawn crackers, onion and chilli rings and coriander leaves. Serve at once.

Serves 3–4
Preparation time: about 40 minutes
Cooking time: about 10 minutes

Spicy Fried Rice

- 125 g/4 oz minced beef
- 1 x 250 g/8 oz can red kidney beans, drained
- 1½ tablespoons nam pla (Thai fish sauce)
- 1 tablespoon dark soy sauce
- 4 red chillies, deseeded and finely chopped
- 3 garlic cloves, crushed
- ½ teaspoon salt
- 2 tablespoons vegetable oil
- 10 green beans, trimmed and cut into 1 cm/½ inch lengths
- 750 g/1½ lb cooked long-grain rice (about 175 g/6 oz raw weight)
- 1 tablespoon sugar
- salt and pepper
- 4 tablespoons roughly chopped fresh basil leaves

1 Put the minced beef and drained kidney beans into a bowl. Mix well and then stir in the nam pla and soy sauce. Cover the bowl and leave to marinate for 30 minutes.

2 Mix the chopped chillies, garlic and salt together in another bowl. Heat the oil in the wok and then add the chilli mixture. Stir-fry briskly for 1 minute.

3 Add the beef and kidney bean mixture to the wok and cook, stirring constantly, for 3 minutes, or until the beef is lightly browned. Add the green beans and stir-fry for 3 further minutes over moderate heat.

4 Stir in the cooked rice and sugar, and cook, stirring, until the rice is hot and all the ingredients are thoroughly mixed. Add salt and pepper or more nam pla to taste if necessary. Mix in the basil leaves, then transfer the spicy fried rice to a warmed serving dish and serve immediately.

Serves 4
Preparation time: 10 minutes
Cooking time: 10 minutes

Recipe Photographers:
Reed International Books Ltd./
GGS Photographics/Graham
Kirk/James Murphy/Clive
Streeter/Philip Webb
Jacket Photographer:
Graham Kirk
Jacket Home Economists:
Lucy Knox and Sarah Lowman